Centennial Remembrance

100 Years...
and Counting

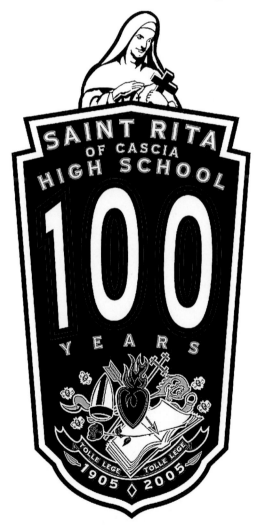

St. Rita of Cascia High School
7740 South Western Avenue
Chicago, Illinois 60620

Printed and bound in the United States of America

Written by Richard P. Bessette for
    St. Rita of Cascia High School
    7740 South Western Avenue
    Chicago, Illinois 60620
    Website: www.stritahs.com

Published by the
    RTN Press, LLC
    P.O. Box 2333
    Orland Park, Illinois 60462
    Website: www.rtnpress.com

Prepared by the
    Five Corners Press
    5052 Route 100
    Plymouth, Vermont 05056
    Website: www.fivecorners.com

Cover Design by:
    Peggy Strocchia, Tim McCarthy, Don Kroitzsh, Rick Bessette

Photograph of Fr. Green on back cover courtesy:
    Chicago Historical Society, Chicago.
    Daily News picture, 1912. DN-0058688

FIRST EDITION
    Second Printing, Summer 2007

Library of Congress Catalog Card Number: 2005900072
ISBN: 0-9747970-1-4

Table Of Contents

St. Rita faculty in 1928. L to R - front row, Fathers Heeney, Albers, Harris, Kepperling, Hammond, Donovan and Maxwell; back row, Fr. Hart, Mr. Connelly, Fr. Martin, Fr. Kirk, Mr. Schlacks and Mr. Jessul.

St. Rita faculty in 1917.

St. Rita faculty in 1910.

St. Rita faculty in 2004. L to R, Fr. Walter McNicholas ('44), Fr. Thomas McCarthy ('83), Br. Jack Hibbard, Br. Jerome Sysko, Fr. Wes Benak ('81), Fr. Bernard Danber ('68) and Br. Gary Hresil ('86).

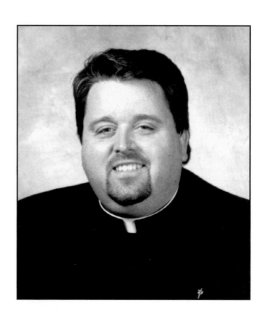

SAINT RITA OF CASCIA HIGH SCHOOL
AN AUGUSTINIAN COLLEGE PREP SCHOOL

Dear Family and Friends of St. Rita High School:

Let me be one of the first to welcome you to our Centennial Celebration; I would like to begin by thanking you for your support of and interest in St. Rita of Cascia High School over the past years. A Centennial Celebration such as ours is a time for thanks and a time for remembrance; thanks for all of our blessings, and remembrance of all our people. And what better way to shout tradition than 100 years of service and devotion to a single mission - the education and development of our young men.

St. Rita High School is truly a faith filled community; a community filled with the wonder of all its people. I am sure each and every one of you - especially the graduates - remember the old buildings with a measure of fondness; we spent our first 85 years at the same location, 63rd and Oakley/Claremont; the last 15 years have been at 77th and Western, two short miles away from the original campus. But, St. Rita High School is so much more than bricks and mortar...it is its people.

Throughout the years thousands of young men have earned the right to call St. Rita their *alma mater* - by last count over 21,000 graduates. These students have been ministered to by almost 300 Augustinian religious, beginning with our founder Father James F. Green back in 1905. In addition to the Augustinians, hundreds of dedicated men and women have shared their time and talent as teachers and coaches at St. Rita. It is the combination of these adults and young men throughout the years that makes St. Rita of Cascia High School what it is...one of the finest high schools in the Nation.

So let's journey together through the pages of this centennial book, keeping in mind all of those who came before us, those that will follow, and how blessed we are to be able to share our memories once again.

May St. Rita of Cascia powerfully intercede for you.

Fr. Tom

Rev. Thomas R. McCarthy, O.S.A. '83
President/Principal

**FOUNDED
1905**

7740 S. WESTERN AVE. CHICAGO, ILLINOIS 60620 PHONE:773-925-6600 FAX:773-925-2451 WWW.STRITAHS.COM

THE AUGUSTINIANS

IN THE WORLD

IN AMERICA

IN CHICAGO

Since its founding in 1837, Chicago was built on the backs of a flood of European immigrants; the Catholic Church in Chicago helped assimilate these masses into the American experience and organized them into a singularly Midwestern parochial system of parishes, churches and schools. Central to this effort was the arrival of various Orders of priests and nuns: from the Jesuits in 1857 and the Christian Brothers in 1861, to the Carmelites in 1900 and the priests and brothers of the Order of St. Augustine shortly thereafter.

James Edward Quigley was named Archbishop of Chicago in 1903, and he promptly set about increasing and improving the parochial school system in the archdiocese. Through Archbishop Quigley's counsel (1903 to 1915) the number of schools increased from 166 to 256, and the number of students from 67,321 to 109,162. Archbishop Quigley had a hand in the founding of two such schools in 1905: the Cathedral College of the Sacred Heart (later renamed Quigley Preparatory Seminary) and another that would be guided by the Augustinians.

Photo courtesy Archdiocese of Chicago's Joseph Cardinal Bernardin Archives and Records Center.

Photo courtesy Chicago Historical Society, Chicago. Daily News picture, 1912. DN-0058688

At the request of Archbishop James E. Quigley (at left) in 1905, the Augustinians, whose motherhouse and sole American province was located in Villanova, Pennsylvania near Philadelphia, were asked to send a foundation group to Chicago. In June of that year Father James F. Green (at right) arrived in Chicago with a vision, a future that would begin on some five acres of land on the sparsely populated southwest side of Chicago. The newest Augustinian Saint – St. Rita of Cascia, who was canonized in 1900 – would be the patroness of the new facility.

While the Augustinian foundation group was new to Chicago and the Midwest, the Order was certainly not new. The lineage of the Augustinians can be traced back to the 6th Century in Europe. Augustine himself did not found the Order but, rather, was known for establishing monasteries and the Rule for monastic life. Over the next six centuries, his followers spread far and wide, building communities throughout Europe that lived under the teachings, writings and example of Augustine. In 1256, Pope Alexander IV presided over a "Grand Union" of a number of the small religious groups, binding them together under a Prior General to channel their forces into an apostolate. Thus, the Augustinians took their place as mendicant friars alongside the Dominicans, the Franciscans and, soon after, the Carmelites. In time the official Order of St. Augustine was born and reborn, through tumultuous times (Martin Luther's Reformation) and quiet periods (Gregor Mendel's research in heredity). The Order accomplished much in the English-speaking world through its' vice-province in Ireland, where Augustinians have triumphed for over seven hundred years; these Irish Augustinians would reach the New World.

Augustinian activity in the United States dates back to the time of George Washington, with the first vice-province chartered in 1796 in Philadelphia; Father Matthew Carr from the Augustinian community in Dublin started the first permanent American settlement at the request of Bishop John Carroll of Baltimore; it was no accident that the Augustinian Prior General in Rome chose the Irish Augustinians from Dublin to pioneer in the New World.

For years, Irish peasant farmers worked tenant farms owned by absentee British landlords, Irish land controlled by England; with no fortunes and little future, the emigration of these peasant farmers to the New World began, a stream that would endure for 100 years. During the four score periods from 1820 through 1900, Ireland would register as one of the top three countries sending its sons and daughters to America; in 182 years of immigration through 2001, almost five million would emigrate from Eire to America, and they would be ministered to in the New World by their own.

What began as an American mission in Philadelphia in 1796 would grow to vice-province that same year, and achieve full provincial status in 1874 as the St. Thomas of Villanova Province. In 1841, Father Patrick Moriarty of the Philadelphia mission arranged for the purchase of 200 acres outside Philadelphia, the genesis of Villanova University.

It was these Irish Augustinians that pioneered in the heavily Irish southside of Chicago when St. Rita was founded; from the Philadelphia Augustinian province, the Chicago foundation took root. With the arrival of Father Green and the Augustinians in 1905, the Parish of St. Rita was founded, and St. Rita High School had its roots. Father Green began the Midwest vice province with St. Rita, the first of what would become three Augustinian based high schools: St. Rita of Cascia, Mendel Catholic and Providence Catholic. The future was clear.

The Chicago area settlement of the Augustinian Order began as a vice province in 1905, and rose to full provincial status in 1941 when it was designated Our Mother of Good Counsel Province, only the second province in the United States. Since reaching full provincial status, the Our Mother of Good Counsel Province has had ten Provincials: Fathers Ruellan P. Fink, Clement C. McHale, John J. Seary, Francis J. Cavanaugh, Leo J. Burke, Raymond R. Ryan, John F. Flynn, Karl A. Gersbach, David L. Brecht and Robert F. Prevost.

Today, the Order of St. Augustine numbers over 2,800 members spread among one Abbey, 26 Provinces, 16 Vicariates and 15 Regions; these encompass hundreds of monasteries in 47 different countries around the globe, all accountable in some fashion to the Prior General.

James Francis Green was born on March 1, 1867 in Chestnut Hill, Pennsylvania, a suburb of Philadelphia; Hugh and Anna (Reilly) Green would be blessed with eight children, James being the firstborn. He attended area grammar and high schools, and showed some interest in pharmacy in his early years. Soon, though, his horizons expanded and he resumed his education, registering for classes at Villanova College in 1884; following college courses, the future Father Green entered the Augustinian Novitiate on August 28, 1887. Fours years later he made his solemn profession as a member of the Augustinian Order; upon completing his course studies in philosophy and theology, he was ordained priest on June 11, 1892 by the Archbishop of Philadelphia.

The new Reverend James F. Green's first assignment was as assistant at St. Mary's Church in Lawrence, Massachusetts, where he remained for almost four years. His second mission was that of the Church of the Immaculate Conception in Hoosick Falls, New York, where he ministered until mid-1898. In July 1898, Father Green was appointed assistant rector of the Augustinian Mission Band (headquartered in Schaghticoke, New York) through which he performed missionary work in many of the larger cities in the United States, including the Archdiocese of Chicago. In 1901, Father Green accepted responsibility for the parish of St. Joseph in Greenwich, New York as his fourth assignment. Now educated, trained and experienced, Father James Francis Green's fifth assignment undoubtedly would be his most challenging and rewarding - the charge to establish the first Augustinian Foundation west of Philadelphia...the future St. Rita – both the parish community and the educational institution.

Just past his 38th birthday, Father Green left New York and headed for Chicago in June 1905. His story in Chicago is well known: establishing the parish and high school of St. Rita of Cascia, laying the cornerstones for three other parish/school missions and, finally, being honored by his fellow Friars when elected to the Board of Definitors of the undivided Province and Vicar Provincial of Illinois.

Father Green held the Order degree of Bachelor of Sacred Theology, the academic degree of Master of Arts from Villanova College (now University), and the honorary degree of Doctor of Laws from Niagara University. He celebrated the Silver Jubilee of his priesthood in 1917. The 69-year old Very Reverend Father James Francis Green entered the house of the Lord on November 3, 1936, having completed 44 years in the priesthood in the Order of St. Augustine.

Rita Lotti is believed to have been born in 1381 in Roccaporena, Italy – in the Province of Umbria near the town of Cascia. She was the only child, and one late in the married life, of the couple Antonio and Amata Lotti; as respected and devout citizens, Rita's parents were the official peacemakers among their people in the neighborhood.

Left to her own devices she leaned toward a religious life as a young woman, but Rita's parents had already arranged a marriage to a man in the area – Paolo Mancini. Arranged marriages were common, and this one was typical of the time; the fact that the marriage also would reconcile some conflicts and family rivalries simply added to the benefits of the arrangement. Thus, she became Rita Lotti Mancini.

The marriage was blessed with two sons, and Rita's life was filled with the daily activities of wife and mother and homemaker. Paolo Mancini was employed in town as a minor civil servant and became drawn into some of the political rivalries; Paolo was ambushed in a vendetta one day. Within a few years, both sons were lost to the ages in separate tragedies. Thus did Rita's life evolve into that of widow and single woman.

As Rita entrusted her life totally to God, she devoted more and more time to charity and prayer. Once again, her desire to have a religious life grew. Rita Lotti Mancini finally tried to join the Augustinian Nuns of Cascia – but was refused entrance. The Augustinian Nuns, who lived at the Monastery of Saint Mary Magdalene, were afraid that their peaceful existence would be upset by accepting a widow with ties to violence and vendettas in the community. But Rita would not accept no.

Reminiscent of the role of her parents and blessed with her own forgiving spirit, Rita worked to reconcile her late husband's family and their rivals; wowed by her inspiration and commitment, the families were reconciled and peace settled over the community. Thus did Rita become Sister Rita on joining the Augustinian Nuns at age 36, living her next forty years according to the Rule of St. Augustine; during the last 15 years of her life, Rita was blessed with a mark of a thorn (stigmata) from Jesus' Crown of Thorns.

The 76-year old Rita Lotti Mancini – Sister Rita – joined her Lord on May 22, 1457, having completed 40 years as a Nun in the Order of St. Augustine. Her life and legend brought her beatification by Pope Urban VIII on October 1, 1627, and canonization by Pope Leo XIII on May 24, 1900. Woman, Wife, Mother, Widow, Nun and Saint.

St. Rita of Cascia

The College

The Parish

The High School

The invitation from Archbishop Quigley to the Augustinian Order to begin a new foundation in Chicago was readily accepted in Philadelphia and Rome; earlier visits by Prior Provincial Father Martin Geraghty had set the stage for this invitation. 38-year old Father James Francis Green arrived in 1905, the Augustinian's first religious superior in the Midwest, and immediately set about the work of establishing the Order's first permanent settlement west of the Mother House.

Five acres of property had been purchased for $33,362 on the southwest side of Chicago, a lightly populated area right in the path of growth; if growth indeed was in the future, the development of the southwest side would come through St. Rita of Cascia. The original plan was to construct three buildings: a monastery, chapel and college. Before the year was out, Father Green had seen the cornerstone laid for St. Rita's College; this initial construction effort resulted in a two-story building (64' by 164') the following year, having cost $36,599; a third story was soon added, for a cost of $17,000. As the first, St. Rita's College housed all the functions of the new mission;

Daily News picture of St. Rita's College, 1912. Photo courtesy Chicago Historical Society, Chicago. DN-0058685

thus began St. Rita High School and the parish of St. Rita. These two would remain inextricably entwined for the next dozen years. While Fr. Green's dream called for educating young men from grammar school through college and included room for the construction of the first Augustinian College west of Philadelphia, his everlasting achievement would be etched in the thousands of young men educated at his high school.

As a Parish, the sparsely settled southwest side of Chicago didn't provide much in the way of parishioners; in 1906, the foundation began with 50-some Catholics in the neighborhood, just seven families. In fact, 17 years earlier this area wasn't even part of Chicago; in 1889 the City of Chicago annexed 100-square miles of territory, effectively doubling it's size. The original parish boundaries were from Damen Avenue to California Street, on the east and west, and from 59th Street on the north with an as-yet-unsettled southern boundary, facing the as-yet-unsettled south side of the

Early class, circa 1911. Back row, Fathers Ford, Green, O'Neill and Egan

City. But the area grew and the boundaries were changed from time to time. Other new parishes were begun in the rapidly expanding frontier of Chicago: St. Nicholas of Tolentine, St. Gall and St. Clare of Montefalco – all in 1909 and all by that pioneering Augustinian - Father Green. Each new parish would build a church and grammar school, which would feed graduates to the high school. In 1911, Father Green purchased five acres for a new St. Rita parish, church and school; in the fall of 1916, the parish grammar school opened with 250 students.

As a high school, St. Rita's College became official in the eyes of the State of Illinois legislature on July 13, 1905. Actual classes began with a group of 14 students in September 1906; Stephen Buckley (the future Monsignor) was the first to enroll, transferring over from Englewood High. While a single student graduated in 1908, the first graduating class would be that of 1909, when four students earned their diplomas. At the beginning, the school offered two different curriculums to the young men of the area: a two-year business course of studies and a four-year college preparatory academic track. J.J. Coppinger is credited with being the first graduate of St. Rita, finishing the business course in 1908. In those early days around 1910, a number of seminarians from Villanova helped teach at the school; one of them would return as Headmaster of St. Rita High School years later. At the turn of the century, Fr. Green probably was the only man with the vision to see that from these small beginnings would grow the largest Catholic all-boys high school in the mid-west.

Three Augustinians formed the nucleus of the Midwest foundation in 1906, Fathers James Green, William Egan and Richard Maher serving as parish priests and school teachers. This arrangement continued for some time, but growth finally overtook the resources available. By 1917 progress in the area had mushroomed to the point where the parish and high school communities had to be split, each to be run separately; thus St. Rita Parish and St. Rita High School began their individual march through time. In 1920, the separate foundations of parish and school were given canonical standing by Rome, thus becoming official. In 1922, Father Green split his duties, becoming pastor of the parish while Father Egan became headmaster of the high school. Both missions continue today, and realize their centennial observance.

Green Hall

Harris Gym

Egan Hall

Monastery

When St. Rita was founded at 63rd and Oakley, it was in the City of Chicago, but only barely so. Looking west from the new school one could only see scrub farmland; Western Avenue formed the westernmost boundary of the Chicago city limits. Looking east wasn't much better, the Baltimore & Ohio railroad tracks being the most visible activity. Looking north one might be able to make out the development heading toward the school; looking south simply viewed open land. The bricks-and-mortar part of building a high school would record the consistent growth of the Augustinian message.

The original building was completed in 1906 and called St. Rita's College, later named Green Hall; it housed the original classrooms (which soon were overtaxed), library, chapel and monastery; a Band room (3rd floor) and athletic locker rooms in the basement followed.

The next construction produced the gymnasium in 1923 (later named Harris Gym); the gym was built onto the west side of the original structure, and had a playing floor measuring 80' by 100'. The Men's Club had room in the basement, as would some of the Technical shops.

This was followed rather quickly in 1926 by a much larger building, with many classrooms and science laboratories (dedicated later as Egan Hall); this new three-story hall was built onto the west side of the gym, and originally was set back from 63rd Street. In 1939 an addition was constructed on the north end of Egan Hall, forming a solid front on 63rd Street.

The last building to front 63rd Street would be the Monastery, completed in 1949. The original quarters for the Augustinians had room for twelve; by 1947 there were 43 religious working at St. Rita and the new Monastery solved the housing problem.

Mendel Technical

Stands/Classrooms

Behind the original College, southward along Oakley Street, a new two-story building was erected to house the Technical Division's machinery and supplies. With auto, diesel and aeronautics shops (1st floor) and electrical/radio/HVAC (2nd floor), this building was dedicated as Mendel Technical in 1938.

Directly behind the buildings on 63rd Street was the school's sports stadium; from a field surrounded by a simple wooden fence, to stands in 1922, it was replaced with a concrete/brick wall (1931) and permanent stands (1946 - 4,000 seats) along Claremont that provided for classroom space under the stands themselves by 1960.

Because of enrollment changes during the 1970's, serious consideration was given to moving the St. Rita High School operation farther south, far away to Tinley Park; while there were pros and cons surrounding the complex issues, in the end the Augustinian Order decided to keep the school at its original location and devoted to its original mission on the southside of Chicago. Then another choice point arrived: while the original facilities served thousands of young men from the Chicago area for 85 years, in order to compete with the more campus-like settings which were in vogue, by 1990 the decision time had come: either invest heavily in plant and equipment at the original location or move the high school to more spacious quarters. St. Rita began serious negotiations with both Sears and the B&O Railroad concerning available property, and then Cardinal Bernardin decided to close Quigley South. With the availability of the Quigley South property (built in 1961 at 7740 South Western Avenue) on 33 acres just two miles south of St. Rita's 63rd Street location, the Augustinian Order moved St. Rita for the first and only time. This move, and the bonding of St. Rita to the southside of Chicago for future generations, was a credit to the courage and foresight of two Ritamen working together: Fr. Bernard Danber ('68) and Jim Segredo ('73).

Photo montage of 77th and Western 33 acre campus of St. Rita

Keeping track of graduates always presents problems, not the least of which is the re-creation of historical records from changing periods. For example, during the war years, St. Rita often had two graduating classes per year, in an effort to speed some young men through the process when they were needed to help arm and defend our Country; in other periods, St. Rita offered two-year, three-year and four-year courses of study. Yet even with these imperfections, in one hundred years of operation, St. Rita High School can boast of graduating over 21,000 young men. While year-by-year numbers are subject to argument, we do have some feel for the approximate totals.

Decade by Decade Graduates	
1900's –	5
1910's –	282
1920's –	417
1930's –	729
1940's –	2,447
1950's –	3,509
1960's –	4,506
1970's –	3,608
1980's –	2,914
1990's –	1,983
2000's –	879
	21,279

The graduation rate experience at St. Rita paralleled that of the entire Archdiocese of Chicago; rising through the early decades of the century, peaking in the 1960's, and falling off through the end of the millennium. This shows that the experience is more than just changing neighborhoods. On an Archdiocese-wide basis, enrollments (which would mimic, but lag graduation rates) in Catholic grammar and high schools peaked at around 366,000 students in 1966; enrollments fell to a little over 111,000 students in the fall of 2003. St. Rita is on a pace to show its first decade-to-decade increase since the 1960's.

LEADERSHIP

Fr. James F. Green, O.S.A.
1905–1922

Fr. William L. Egan, O.S.A.
1922–1926

Fr. Joseph B. Kepperling, O.S.A.
1926–1929

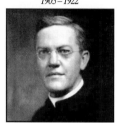

Fr. John J. Harris, O.S.A.
1929–1935

Fr. Ruellan P. Fink, O.S.A.
1935–1956

Leadership is a funny quality; while education certainly helps improve your ability, one simply cannot learn leadership from a book. St. Rita has been blessed with wonderful leadership for 100 years, beginning with its Founder Father Green and leading through fourteen other men up to today.

As the focus of activity in what would become the Our Mother of Good Counsel Province, practically every single Augustinian who ventured west would spend some time at St. Rita High School, working with and helping form the young men of the day.

Father Green's story now is a familiar one, having founded the Parish and College in 1905. Father Green remained at the high school through 1922, at which time he began to focus his energies on the Parish. Father Green's tenure spanned a world at war.

Father Egan, who came to the high school soon after its founding and remained as a teacher, was raised to Rector of St. Rita High School when the Founder left. It was Father Egan who led the school through growth and building in the Roaring 20's.

Father Kepperling became the Third Rector/Principal of the high school in 1926. Father Kepperling had been at St. Rita as a Villanova seminarian around 1910, helping out with the teaching duties. This, then, was his second stint at the high school. His early demise was a loss for the school.

Father Harris worked at St. Rita for years, many of them as what is now referred to as the Athletic Director. After years in the classroom, Father Harris became Principal in 1929 and stayed on through the darkest periods of the Depression.

Father Fink would enjoy the longest tenure of any Rector; he was handed a struggling mission at the end of the Depression and did not stop investing his time and talent until it was a bustling enterprise bursting with students 21 years later, even with World War II and Korea.

Father McLaughlin took the reins in 1956 and masterfully steered the community for the next six years. This was a period of recovery from the war and unprecedented buildup of jobs and inflation from the pent up demand. It was a changing world.

Fr. John E. McLaughlin, O.S.A.
1956–1962

Fr. Francis P. Crawford, O.S.A.
1962–1968

Fr. Daniel B. Trusch, O.S.A.
1968–1971

Fr. LaVern J. Flach, O.S.A.
1971–1979

Fr. David L. Brecht, O.S.A.
1979–1983

Father Crawford had the pleasure and privilege of leading the charge of St. Rita through a most interesting period - the 60's. It began with suburban sprawl and ended with racial change; the Kennedy brothers and Martin Luther King were on the national stage.

Father Trusch rose to Rector at the end of the 1960's, right at the buildup in Vietnam and all that implied for the youth of the day. War, jobs and inflation were still the issues of the day, and St. Rita High School ministered to those needs. Man went to the moon.

Father Flach's tenure saw the escalation and end of hostilities in Vietnam, and the resignation of a President. OPEC became a concern of every household. The Personal Computer arrived, and education at St. Rita changed with the times.

Father Brecht caught the beginning of Generation X, but handled the transition of school and student with aplomb. St. Rita returned to its original mission of preparing young men for college, mirroring the changing field of education and technology.

Father Murphy ('66) accepted the mantle of Rector in 1983, the first alumnus to do so. Chernobyl and Challenger would occupy the news, while the Berlin Wall came tumbling down; through all, St. Rita equipped yet another new generation of young men for the future.

Father Danber ('68, the 2nd alumni Rector) mastered change, St. Rita moving from its home of 85 years to a new campus two miles away. It was the age of Bart Simpson and the Hubble space telescope. St. Rita never lost sight of its charge – preparation and education of young men.

Father O'Connor became St. Rita's first President, as the school changed administrative styles in 1993; separating administration from academics would allow distinction in both. The Chicago Bulls showed their distinction, notching two triples in 8 years.

Mr. Bamberger was the other half of the new administrative arrangement, becoming the first lay Principal in 1993. Mr. Bamberger guided the high school course of studies to academic excellence – judged one of the top high schools by U.S. News & World Report.

In 2000 Father McCarthy ('83) became the second President, and the Fourteenth and current Principal in 2002; a new man for a new millennium. While mapping the human genome is the science du jour, St. Rita High School retains its educational lineage, even after 100 years.

Fr. Patrick E. Murphy, O.S.A.
1983 – 1989

Fr. Bernard R. Danber, O.S.A.
1989 – 1993

Fr. Michael J. O'Connor, O.S.A.
1993 – 2000

Mr. Joseph F. Bamberger
1993 – 2002

Fr. Thomas R. McCarthy, O.S.A.
2000 – Current

1900's 1910's 1920's 1930's 1940's 1950's 1960's 1970's 1980's 1990's 2000's

Graduating Classes

1908 – 1
1909 – 4

1900's – The 12th Census of the U.S. showed 76 million people; eight million immigrants poured through Ellis Island. The Union grew to 46 states; William McKinley was assassinated; Teddy Roosevelt made the 1900's a period of trust busting. It began as a prosperous time; later, many Americans left to work on the Panama Canal. 95 percent of the population still lived on farms. AM radio, the Ford Model T and the Rose Bowl debuted. O'Henry started writing, Caruso making music. 25-mph electric trolley cars invaded the inner city of Chicago; the only all-Chicago World Series took place. Pope Pius X (now Saint) led the Church (1903-14); James E. Quigley was appointed Archbishop of Chicago (1903-15), the 2nd. By 1908, Chicago Catholic schools, elementary and secondary, numbered 125 with enrollment around 80,000.

Original two-story St. Rita's College... Note on the original building that the Oakley Street steps, where scores of students would have their pictures taken, have not been finished; indeed, Oakley Street doesn't yet seem passable.

...jump ahead a few years at St. Rita and a third floor has been added to the original structure; note that while the Oakley Street steps have been finished, Oakley Street itself still isn't much of a thoroughfare.

St. Rita founded by Father Green 1905

Bishop Muldoon dedicates 1st building 1906

St. Rita opens with 14 students 1906

1900's 1910's 1920's 1930's 1940's 1950's 1960's 1970's 1980's 1990's 2000's

Remember When
323-acre Marquette Park
opens in 1906

Thought to be the oldest school picture - dated 1908; begins the tradition of pictures on the Oakley Street steps.

St. Rita fields its first football team 1908	St. Rita graduates its 1st student 1908	First official graduating class 1909

1900's **1910's** 1920's 1930's 1940's 1950's 1960's 1970's 1980's 1990's 2000's

Graduating Classes

1910 – 21
1911 – 24
1912 – 24
1913 – 24
1914 – 34
1915 – 35
1916 – 33
1917 – 27
1918 – 32
1919 – 28

1910's – The Union grew to 48 states, led by Woodrow Wilson. There were no cures for infectious diseases like smallpox, scarlet fever and diphtheria; influenza struck and killed over 20 million in under a year. With millions of men drawn from the labor pool for the War effort, a great migration to the industrial north began. A war economy built up momentum, and ended with a period of stimulation and high spirits – the onset of the Roaring 1920's. Notre Dame invented the forward pass, and the Indianapolis 500 started. The groundwork for the suffrage movement was laid. The subject of "wet" versus "dry" party platforms and States began…leading to Prohibition. A new Pope - Benedict XV (1914-22); Chicago welcomed its new Archbishop (1915-39), George Mundelein, who would become its first Cardinal Priest (1924).

School picture, 1909/10 Class; Frs. Reilly, Green and Gallagher, front center.

| Dominican nuns to OSA Mission Schools 1910 | St. Rita student body reaches 144 1911 | St. Rita graduates its 1st four-year class 1911 |

Did You Know
Graduation Ceremonies
1913 Linden Theatre
1914 Englewood Theatre
1915 Harvard Theatre

Ernest W. Thiele (1895-1993) was a graduate of the Class of 1912, one of only 24 that year. Witness to the scientific explosion of the early 20th century, Ernie would go on to great things in a storied career. After St. Rita, Ernie attended Loyola University (AB), the University of Illinois (BS) and Massachusetts Institute of Technology (MS and PhD). Beginning a 35-year career in research at Standard Oil of Indiana, Ernie was on loan to the University of Chicago during World War II to work on the Manhattan Project - working on heavy water extraction. His life's work in chemical engineering led to 17 publications and 27 patents. After retirement from the oil company, Ernie taught for ten years at Notre Dame. Thiele is immortalized by a Thiele Lecture Series at Notre Dame and an annual Thiele Award by the American Institute of Chemical Engineers.

Tom Dower was a graduate of the Class of 1910 - one of only 21 in that early class. Tom went on to a very successful career in business, culminating in his Presidency of Russell Packing, a large meat packer located in Chicago; Tom Dower also had successful forays in the banking business, becoming President of Peerless Investment, and Chairman of Evergreen Plaza Bank, now a division of Suburban Bank. Tom always had a soft spot in his heart for Catholic education and he made sure gifts from his estate would aid institutions supporting his causes for years to come; toward that end, he established the Thomas W. Dower Foundation which continues to fund Catholic education today - including St. Rita High School.

Land in Marquette Manor for new St. Rita parish 1911

Francis McGrority gets 1st St. Rita scholarship 1913

New St. Rita parish facilities started 1915

The youngest of three brothers to attend St. Rita (J. Lee ('11) and Ed ('12)), Joseph Merrion (1898-1971) was one of 33 graduates from the Class of 1916. Fresh out of St. Rita, Joe went into the building trades; over time, he became a real estate developer in his own right, and one of some note. Born and raised on the south side of Chicago around 56th and Peoria (Visitation parish), Joe's work would follow the growth on the south side all the way through the south suburbs. One of his early projects was a development named Merrionette Manor on the southeast side; he began by filling in wetlands with slag from the mills, and then built duplexes on the property to satisfy the post World War II boom; property also was set aside for a Catholic church, which resulted in Our Lady Gate of Heaven. Joe's work eventually would include large developments in Hometown and Country Club Hills, besides having one named after the family business - Merrionette Park. Joe was a founding member of the National Association of Home Builders, and was honored for his philanthropic work by being named a Knight of St. Gregory by the Vatican in the 1950's. He is shown, above, in a formal picture and, below, with his sister Gert flanking Eleanor (Sis) Daley and Chicago's Mayor Richard J. Daley.*

Malachy P. Foley (1896-1977) was a St. Rita graduate from the Class of 1915 - one of 35; Malachy came from Nativity parish in Chicago, won a scholarship to St. Rita, captained the baseball team, and graduated valedictorian of the Class of 1915. After St. Rita he attended St. Mary's Seminary in Baltimore, Maryland and then the Sulpician Seminary at Catholic University in Washington, D.C.; he was ordained by Archbishop George Mundelein at Holy Name Cathedral on December 23, 1922. With a strong call to service, Malachy eventually became the Very Reverend Monsignor Malachy P. Foley. Monsignor Foley earned B.A., M. A. and S.T.B. degrees from St. Mary's in Baltimore; he was awarded a LLD from Villanova in 1941, a LittD from DePaul in 1942 and a LLD from Loyola in 1969. His life's work included that of Professor at Quigley Seminary, Chaplain for Academy of Our Lady, Rector of Quigley Seminary, Rector of St. Mary of the Lake Seminary in Mundelein and Pastor of St. Bride. He was accorded the honors of Papal Chamberlain (1938), Censor Librorum (1938), Papal Domestic Prelate (1947) and Protonotary Apostolic (1957). Monsignor Foley just missed reaching his 55th anniversary in the priesthood.

Augustinian educators at St. Rita, school year 1915/16. L to r, Frs. J.J. Barthouski, J.B. Kepperling, unidentified, J.M. Fagan, W.L. Egan, J.F. Green, unidentified, C.J. Ford, P.F. Healey, J.A. Perkins, A.M. Martel and unidentified.

| New St. Rita parish school opens 1916 | St. Rita accredited by Illinois Board of Education 1917 | St. Rita parish and high school split 1917 |

1900's **1910's** 1920's 1930's 1940's 1950's 1960's 1970's 1980's 1990's 2000's

School picture, 1916/17 Class; Frs. Egan and Green behind small child with dog.

Monsignor Patrick Brennan (1900-1950) was educated at St. Rita's until 1917. He attended Quigley Preparatory until 1922 and Mundelein Seminary until 1928, when he was ordained a priest for the Archdiocese of Chicago. After work for some years in the archdiocese, he joined the Columban Order of missionaries in 1936, and went to Korea a year later. He was one of many expelled from Korea as enemy aliens in 1942; Monsignor Patrick became an Army chaplain during World War II, served during the Normandy invasion and the battle in the Ardennes, and was decorated for bravery. In 1946 he returned to his missionary work in Korea; he was appointed Prefect Apostolic of Kwangju, Korea by the Holy See in 1948. With other missionaries, he was imprisoned by North Korean troops in July, 1950; it is believed he died in prison in September, 1950; he was 49 years old.

Edward J. Barrett (1900-1977) graduated from the Class of 1917 and, other than stints in the armed forces during both world wars, spent practically all of his life in politics. In fact, it is believed that Ed holds the distinction of being the only public official to hold three different elective offices in state government: Illinois State Treasurer (1931-1933), Auditor of Public Accounts (1933-1941) and Secretary of State (1945-1953). After state government, Ed joined the Cook County government and served five terms as Cook County Clerk (1955-1973) under Mayor Richard J. Daley. Ed served in the Army in World War I and in the Marines in World War II.

| 1st talks of a new Midwestern Province 1918 | New St. Rita parish church opens 1918 | Catholic League in football is formed 1919 |

1900's 1910's **1920's** 1930's 1940's 1950's 1960's 1970's 1980's 1990's 2000's

Graduating Classes

1920 – 30
1921 – 20
1922 – 33
1923 – 53
1924 – 32
1925 – 31
1926 – 60
1927 – 52
1928 – 64
1929 – 42

1920's – The former Allies would experience peace and prosperity; Germany financial ruin and disgrace. The 14th Census of the U.S. population showed 106 million people; quotas would be placed on immigration. America went sports crazy. It was the Jazz Age; Louis Armstrong made music. Movies went from silent to talkie. The economy charged ahead until the Crash in 1929. Gains in the agriculture would not match those of industry; over half the population lived in city centers, instead of on farms. The decade ended with the stock market crash, bank runs, and a credit crunch; fuel for the Great Depression. Calvin Coolidge had inherited an economy on the rebound and handed off one on the brink of collapse; Herbert Hoover couldn't stop it. Pius XI was the new Pope; he would lead for 17 years (1922-39).

William J. Campbell (1905-1988) was a graduate of 1922, out of a class of 33 young men. Bill was but one of many St. Rita graduates who would go on to distinction in legal circles. Bill attended Loyola University, where he received LLB and LLM degrees. Appointed Judge in 1940 by President Franklin Delano Roosevelt, William Campbell would serve more than 30 years on the United States District Court, rising to Chief Judge in 1959. His period on the bench was marked by landmark issues of the day and some that were carried out on a national stage, like the Chicago 7 affair at the 1968 Democratic National Convention.

St. Rita's baseball field was in the southwest corner of the sports stadium behind the school; picture dates to 1922.

Fr. J. Harris made
Athletic Director
1920

St. Rita accredited
by North Central
Association 1921

St. Rita Stadium
built behind
school 1922

1900's 1910's **1920's** 1930's 1940's 1950's 1960's 1970's 1980's 1990's 2000's

While St. Rita High School celebrates its 100th Anniversary, some of its graduates prepare for their own centennial... case in point - Bill Hillmert from the Class of 1924. Shown below and above at left in his graduation pictures; Mr. Hillmert is shown above at right in a current picture. Bill was an accomplished violinist and, at graduation from St. Rita, received the Gold Medal for General Excellence in 4th Year Students. The legacy continues, as his grandson Bill graduated in 2000.

Sports in the Roaring '20's. Shown above is the 1926 flyweight basketball team...knee pads and all. Below, the 1926 St. Rita track team that won the Catholic High School Special 1/2 Mile Relay in 1:37.6 (defeating Loyola and St. Ignatius) at the Marquette Relays in Milwaukee on May 9, 1926; l to r, "Pie" Cranley, O'Hara, Murphy and Lauferski.

Bill Hillmert ('24)

Father Kepperling, front and center, with Senior Class.

Remember When
Forerunner to Marquette Bank
opens at 63rd & Western in 1925.

St. Rita wins it's
1st baseball title
1922

Father Egan
becomes St. Rita's
2nd Rector 1922

2nd building done
(later Harris Gym)
1923

1900's 1910's **1920's** 1930's 1940's 1950's 1960's 1970's 1980's 1990's 2000's

Class of 1927 Student Council

W.J. Linklater
President

L.R. Cella
Secretary

J.C. Evans
Vice President

G.B. Stalzer
Treasurer

T.A. Shields

A.R. Rudcki

~ **Class 1927** ~

Remember When
Colony Theatre opens @
59th & Kedzie in 1925.

St. Rita's version of the Brady Bunch was bigger, and had a lot of men. The senior Brady was John F. from the Class of 1926; he and his wife Florence would be blessed with 10 children, seven of them boys, and all of them Ritamen. Shown in a 1992 picture, Fr. Bernard Danber honored the family during a football game at St. Rita. Next to Fr. Danber were Florence and John F. The seven sons who would call St. Rita their alma mater were: John W. ('52), James J. ('55), Robert E. ('58), Thomas M. ('63), William P. ('67), Daniel J. ('70) and Michael D. ('73).

Did You Know
Carl Cronin ('27) was elected to the Canadian Football Hall of Fame?

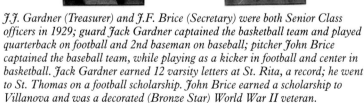

J.J. Gardner (Treasurer) and J.F. Brice (Secretary) were both Senior Class officers in 1929; guard Jack Gardner captained the basketball team and played quarterback on football and 2nd baseman on baseball; pitcher John Brice captained the baseball team, while playing as a kicker in football and center in basketball. Jack Gardner earned 12 varsity letters at St. Rita, a record; he went to St. Thomas on a football scholarship. John Brice earned a scholarship to Villanova and was a decorated (Bronze Star) World War II veteran.

St. Rita State and City football champion 1923	St. Rita begins the Cascian (later, the Ritan) Oct. 1923	3rd building done (later Egan Hall) 1926

1900's 1910's **1920's** 1930's 1940's 1950's 1960's 1970's 1980's 1990's 2000's

St. Rita versus Mt. Carmel in the snow at St. Rita stadium, November 19, 1927; note SRO on Visitor's side; picture by Chicago Architectural M-6350. The St. Rita versus Mt. Carmel game played at St. Rita in front of 8,000 fans on October 1, 2004 was the 80th meeting of these two powerhouses.

Mel Schreier ('28) attended De Paul University after graduating from St. Rita; he earned a BA and an MA in History. But, like many of his era, Mel's working life started before he graduated from high school; as a senior at St. Rita, Mel started work for the Daily Racing Form...the bible of thoroughbred horse racing; his career at the DRF would last 52 years and he would retire as Midwest Editor.

Class of 1924 celebrating their 5th Reunion

Did You Know
Robert Keeley ('27) founded the Pediatrics Department at Mercy Hospital in Chicago?

Remember When
Coached by Fred Dillon, Chicago De LaSalle won it's first National Catholic Interscholastic Basketball Championship in 1929, but not until it got by St. Rita by a score of 12 to 9 after Coach "Hicks" Connelly put in the "figure 8" stall.

| Father Kepperling becomes St. Rita's 3rd Rector 1926 | Predecessor to Mother's Club begins 1929 | Father Harris becomes St. Rita's 4th Rector 1929 |

1900's 1910's 1920's **1930's** 1940's 1950's 1960's 1970's 1980's 1990's 2000's

Graduating Classes

1930 – 49
1931 – 57
1932 – 48
1933 – 88
1934 – 92
1935 – 69
1936 – 75
1937 – 79
1938 – 89
1939 – 83

1930's – Stalin/Hitler/Mussolini/Roosevelt/Chiang/Mao/Hirohito made preliminary moves. Roosevelt's "New Deal" encompassed Reform, Recovery and Relief; the Dust Bowl piled on. With flaws in capitalism showing, radical Communists started the red scare. Talk of ending Prohibition gained favor; the five-day workweek became more prevalent. Rural electrification gained; new federal highways spread suburban development. Art Deco arrived; George Burns & Gracie Allen hit radio; the Gershwins made musicals, Billie Holliday and the Dorsey's music. Gone With the Wind hit the big screen. Jay Berwanger won the 1st Heisman, the Blackhawks their 1st Stanley. Pope Pius XII began leading the Church (1939-58); Chicago gained a new Archbishop (1939-58), Samuel Stritch, who in 1946 would become its 2nd Cardinal Priest.

Remember When
Flys under 118 lbs
Bantams 118 to 132
Lights 133 to 150
Heavies 150 and up

Did You Know
Raleigh Kean ('30) and his brother Lawrence ('28) founded Kean Brothers Oil Company; they built the firm from a home heating oil company into a string of gas stations on the south side of Chicago.

Remember When
Weekly Mass for the whole student body was on Wednesday's at 8:30 with Fr. Harris presiding.

The friendly confines of St. Rita Stadium, late 1920's/early 1930's; the yet-to-be-named Egan Hall is seen at upper right, the wooden stands at left.

St. Rita celebrates
25th Anniversary
1930

Earliest Yearbook
takes the name
Cascian 1930

Forerunner to
Father's Club
36 men - 1930

1900's 1910's 1920's **1930's** 1940's 1950's 1960's 1970's 1980's 1990's 2000's

Senior Class Officers in 1932. L to r, Pat Donovan, Ed Prairie, Matt Foley and John Muellman.

Bill Murphy - or to be exact - Fr. William P. Murphy, O.S.A. ('33), a man you should know. He was ordained in 1943 and, after a number of ministries over the years, was named Pastor of Queen of Martyrs Parish in 1973. Pastor for the next twelve years, he helped Queen of Martyrs retire its debt and refurbish its facilities; he became Pastor Emeritus in 1986, and still resides at Queen of Martyrs. The Order of St. Augustine honored him with the Filiis Ordinis Award.

Will Lang ('32) was another in the long line of Ritamen to make his alma mater proud. At St. Rita, Will quarterbacked the football team and, as a senior, was captain of the basketball team; he wrote for the Ritan and Cascian. After graduation, Will kept at his writing work. He became a World War II correspondent serving in Major General Matthew B. Ridgeway's All American Division - the 82nd Airborne. Eventually, Will became Bureau Chief for Life *magazine. He is shown at left in his basketball uniform.*

When the camera was moved to the westside hashmark, Harris Gym and Green Hall became visible; Mendel Tech did not yet exist on the Visitor's side.

| Library enlarged by a factor of six 1930 | Concrete wall surrounds football field 1931 | Father Fink becomes St. Rita's 5th Rector 1935 |

1900's 1910's 1920's **1930's** 1940's 1950's 1960's 1970's 1980's 1990's 2000's

Brothers Jim and Mike Flannery graduated from St. Rita in 1934 and 1935, respectively. Jim went on to marry and father eight children - seven of them boys and all of them Ritamen. At left, from l to r, Rob ('61), Jim ('63), Mike ('64), Pat ('66), Maggie (who attended Maria), Kevin ('69), John ('71) and Tom ('74). The picture dates to March, 1961 so the three boys on the left - Rob, Jim and Mike - were in senior, sophomore and freshman year at St. Rita when the picture was taken. The lone woman, Maggie, did her share for the School, marrying a Ritaman and sending her son to St. Rita. The third generation of Flannery's now has started - Sean Patrick graduating in 2002.

At right, this undated photograph shows a corner of the General Study Hall.
Below, ever the showman, Father Green was given the honor of driving the trolley as the move from horses to electricity was celebrated.

Earl Evans ('30), one of the real patriarchs of St. Rita; from his extended family we can trace 28 St. Rita alumni and current students still working their way through St. Rita.

Founding Pastor
Father Green
passes away 1936

1906 building
named Green Hall
1936

Fr. Potter begins
Technical Course
offerings 1936

1900's 1910's 1920's **1930's** 1940's 1950's 1960's 1970's 1980's 1990's 2000's

John Madigan ('34) was a successful journalist and newscaster in Chicago and Washington, D.C. for more than fifty years. He covered Presidential conventions and campaigns from 1940 to 1988, when he retired from the journalism part of his career; not quite ready for full retirement, he began a stint as Press Officer for the Illinois Supreme Court that lasted for another decade. John served in the Navy during World War II, and stays near the water today, splitting his time between Grand Beach, Michigan and Lauderhill, Florida. John is shown above in a 2004 picture, at age 86. He remembers deciding on a career as a newsman in junior year at St. Rita, thanks to two teachers: Mr. John Waldron and Fr. John Seary.

Did You Know
Fr. Paul Potter, who started the Technical Courses at St. Rita in the 1930's was the reserve Chaplain of the U.S. Air Corps detachment at Municipal (Midway) airport.

Remember
Egan Hall Rooms
103/104?

Remember When
Each student was asked to contribute 2 cents weekly to the Society for the Propagation of the Faith...and the late charge in the Library was 2 cents/day.

Remember 3 Athletic Fields
One behind school
One on NE corner of 63rd & Oakley
One on SE corner of 65th & Bell

Here is a man you should know - Desmond Coleman. Mr. Coleman began his affiliation with St. Rita in 1928; he began teaching soon after, and retired from active teaching in 1975...a 45 year run. Des made it a semi-retirement and stayed on at the school for a few more years helping out with Administration. Among other things, he was in charge of the summer school program and the eighth grade entrance exams. Mr. Coleman was given the Filiis Ordinis *Award by the Augustinian Order.*

Whether you walked, rode or took public transportation, the end of the day was a mad rush.

Mendel Technical building opens 1938	Egan Hall extended north to front 63rd 1939	St. Rita begins a summer school program 1939

1900's 1910's 1920's 1930's **1940's** 1950's 1960's 1970's 1980's 1990's 2000's

Graduating Classes

1940 – 169
1941 – 204
1942 – 231
1943 – 215
1944 – 213
1945 – 179
1946 – 292
1947 – 309
1948 – 309
1949 – 326

1940's – The 16th Census of the U.S. showed 132 million people. When France fell, the U.S. could field only 5 divisions; Germany had 140; rationing began; the atom bomb arrived. At the end of the war, the USSR and the U.S. divided Korea along the 38th parallel; the Allies divided Europe and Germany. After Williams and DiMaggio played in 1941, professional sports dropped from view; when the war ended, sports exploded as stars returned. Penicillin was perfected; streptomycin followed and the age of wonder drugs was born. The economy soared, price controls followed. The GI Bill of Rights provided college education and subsidized new homes, fashioning the great middle class. Irving Berlin, Glenn Miller and Perry Como made music; *Oklahoma* hit Broadway. *The Lone Ranger* was on TV, Groucho Marx on radio.

Edmund Rooney ('42) was another Rita grad who would make his fame and fortune writing. Ed was a reporter for the Chicago Daily News *for 26 years; he helped the* News *win a Pulitzer Prize for Public Service in 1957, reporting on fraud in government. He would eventually earn his Ed.D. and become a professor at Loyola University in Chicago. He also contributed articles for the Alumni Newsletter of St. Rita for years.*

Remember When
School Telephones: Prospect 3014-3015

William T. Doyle ('41) lettered in football at St. Rita and also ran track; in fact, it is football where he is remembered since his generosity financed a large part of the new stadium, which carries his name - Doyle Stadium. After high school Bill got started in the grocery business, which would lead to his owning a string of supermarkets - Sunshine Supermarkets. Bill would parlay that investment into an interest in the 1st National Bank of Sturgis *(Michigan); 14 years later he would raise the stakes and gain an interest in the* Campbell Fetter Bank *of Kendalville, Indiana; he would rise to Chairman of both.*

Ken Schuster ('44) won his monogram at Notre Dame as a 215 lbs. 6'2" left tackle (#70) after leaving St. Rita, one of roughly 2,600 to make the official all-time roster. Ken eventually went to work for Central Steel & Wire *where he stayed for 45 years, the last 19 as Chairman. He is shown as a St. Rita student, a Notre Dame student and as he looks today.*

St. Rita begins twice a year graduations 1940

Our Mother of Good Counsel Province 1941

St. Rita debt free for 1st time 1942

1900's 1910's 1920's 1930's **1940's** 1950's 1960's 1970's 1980's 1990's 2000's

Everyone makes a difference, but some leave a bigger wake as they pass by: Fr. Walter F. McNicholas OSA is one such man who has touched many. L to r: a fresh graduate from St. Rita on D-Day June 6, 1944 - since there were no yearbooks in 1943/44/45, his July 1944 Navy picture dates shortly after graduation; a 1968 photograph early in his career as teacher at St. Rita; lastly, a 2004 picture showing his celebration of 35 years at St. Rita, besides 60 years from graduation and 51 years as priest in the Order of St. Augustine.

Remember When
Fr. Fink would come on School speaker system with the introduction "Students of the Institute!"

That's Maurice O'Connor ('43) next to Illinois Governor Dwight Green in 1942 watching a football game.

Remember When
Weekly Mass @8:30am
Freshmen – Monday
Sophomores – Tuesday
Juniors – Wednesday
Seniors - Friday

Remember When
Father Joseph Burns was disciplinarian and "jug master?"

The aeronautics department of the Technical School; how the airplanes got to St. Rita's field is another story. Pictures from Spring, 1945; l to r, a Stinson Vigilant (Tony Studin '45 in the pilot's seat); a Curtis AT9; the open cowl of the right engine on the AT9. This was Fr. Cibulskis' class.

188 of 231 in Class of 1942 serve in WW II

1st issue of Alumni News 1941/42

St. Rita Alumni Association formed 1944

1900's 1910's 1920's 1930's **1940's** 1950's 1960's 1970's 1980's 1990's 2000's

This undated photograph by Chicago Architectural *shows St. Rita's Chapel in the original Green Hall.*

Jim Miller ('47) has had a long and successful business career since attending St. Rita. With degrees from Northwestern and the University of Chicago, Jim was brought in to Intermatic Corporation in 1970 as CEO during a time of transition; after making Malibu Lights a household name, he rose to Chairman. Today he is Chairman of the Board of Qualitas Manufacturing.

Remember When
New Planet Roller Rink at 7534 Racine
White City Roller Rink at 345 East 63rd

The new Monastery for the Augustinians was on the rise in this picture dated May 18, 1948; the picture was taken by St. Rita junior John Tyma, who in time would become Fr. John Tyma, OSA; Fr. Tyma currently serves in Trujillo, Peru. The picture was saved and sent in by Fr. Daniel Hartigan.

| Fire destroys St. Rita football stadium 1944 | Concrete football stands for 2,000 1946 | Ground broken for new Monastery 1947 |

1900's 1910's 1920's 1930's **1940's** 1950's 1960's 1970's 1980's 1990's 2000's

Senior Prom at Medina Country Club (5/7/48), attended by 220 couples. Picture shows the traditional Grand March of the Seniors, halfway through the night. At lower left is Mike O'Grady, who worked on the Ritan.

Remember When
Bowling had two leagues – a Thursday and a Friday league, and the leading teams had names like the Big Five, the Pouncers and the Ricksters?

School's out - 1949.

St. Rita High School
Commencement Exercises
Colony Theatre
Fifty-ninth Street and Kedzie Avenue
Wednesday, June the first
Nineteen hundred and forty-nine
Two o'clock   Admit One
―――――――――――――――――――――――
(Theatre will not be opened before 1:15 P.M.)
622

Wheels and teenagers, a decades old tradition; in this 1946 picture, l to r, Schuette ('?), Len Sarnacki ('49) and George Raphael ('49).

Drafting class - circa late-1940's.

| St. Rita introduces its Marching Band 1947 | St. Rita institutes driver's training course 1948 | Monastery opened for Augustinians 1949 |

1900's 1910's 1920's 1930's 1940's **1950's** 1960's 1970's 1980's 1990's 2000's

Graduating Classes

1950 – 333
1951 – 325
1952 – 328
1953 – 381
1954 – 367
1955 – 395
1956 – 387
1957 – 364
1958 – 176
1959 – 453

1950's – Korea was at war; Vietnam was partitioned. Alaska and Hawaii rounded out the Union. *I Love Lucy*, *Ozzie and Harriet*, *TV Guide*, and Soaps arrived. "Buddy" Holly, Ritchie Valens and the Big Bopper ended their rock and roll career. Elvis Presley signed with RCA, and the U.S. Army. Tylenol competed with aspirin. Scientists developed a hydrogen bomb, decoded DNA, postulated superconductivity, eradicated polio, built the laser, entered space and transplanted organs. Mantle, Mays and Aaron were rookies; Marciano undefeated. Eisenhower/Nixon ran for the White House. Chevrolet rolled-out the Corvette, Ford the Edsel. Brown vs. Board of Education ended public school segregation; Federal troops went to Little Rock. 42-year old Rosa Parks just said no; 26-year old Martin Luther King, Jr. stepped on the national stage. *Nautilus* voyaged under the North Pole. Pope John XIII began his short (1958-63) but groundbreaking Papacy; Chicago received Albert Meyer, its 3rd leader (1958-65) who would rise to Cardinal Priest.

John F. O'Toole ('53) went into the advertising business after completing his education...and it wasn't wasted. He rose to Chairman of advertising giant Foote, Cone & Belding.

1950/51 Courses of Study
Academic
Scientific
Technical or Pre-Engineering
Business Administration

Father Joe Hennessey's Woodshop.

St. Rita Chicago
Baseball League
Champion 1951

St. Rita basketball
City Champion
1952

OSA's start 2nd
Chicago-area HS
- Mendel 1951/52

1900's 1910's 1920's 1930's 1940's **1950's** 1960's 1970's 1980's 1990's 2000's

Here is a pair of Ritamen you should know. Pat Mahoney, on the left, and Mike McArdle, on the right - both from the Class of 1954. In fact, both is a good word with these two: they both went to De Paul Law School, they both were admitted to the Illinois Bar in 1961, they both practice in downtown Chicago, they both named their first born sons Tim, they both are in the St. Rita Hall of Fame, they both were founding members of the St. Rita Board of Advisors, they both were given the Filiis Ordinis Award by the Augustinian Order and they both are loyal Ritamen...these two Irishmen remain fast friends.

1951 - St. Rita's Driver's Ed. dual-control car, supplied by McManus Chevrolet.

*Ray Manczarek ('56), who gained fame with the **DOORS** and entered the Rock & Roll Hall of Fame in 1993, didn't make the St. Rita band. He graduated from DePaul University, went to Los Angeles, met Jim Morrison and cut **Light My Fire**.*

John Husar graduated in the 50th Anniversary Class of 1955; he loved writing and the outdoors, and managed to blend the two into a career. John was the Outdoor Editor for the Chicago Tribune for years.

1905   1955

The Augustinian Fathers
request the honor of your presence at the
Solemn Pontifical Mass of Thanksgiving
commemorating the
Golden Jubilee of the Founding
of
Saint Rita of Cascia High School
His Excellency
The Most Reverend Peter Canisius van Lierde, O.S.A.
Titular Bishop of Porphyreon
Sacristan and Vicar General of His Holiness for Vatican City
will pontificate at eleven o'clock in the
Church of Saint Rita
Chicago, Illinois
and you are cordially invited to attend the
Golden Jubilee Banquet
at the
Conrad Hilton Hotel
at eight o'clock in the evening
Tuesday, October the eighteenth
One thousand nine hundred and fifty-five
His Eminence Samuel Cardinal Stritch
Archbishop of Chicago
will preside

R. s. v. p.

Steel Football stands added on East side 1953

Classrooms built under stadium seats 1954

St. Rita celebrates 50th Anniversary 1955

1900's 1910's 1920's 1930's 1940's **1950's** 1960's 1970's 1980's 1990's 2000's

After St. Rita, Art Velasquez ('56) attended Notre Dame (BSEE) and the University of Chicago (MBA); he is a founder of Azteca Corn Products *which was sold to and rebought from* Pillsbury Company, *mirroring the dealmaking that went on in the 1980's. Besides being the first Hispanic elected to a statewide office, Art has been a board member and advisor to many corporations and charities, and remains a loyal friend of St. Rita.*

Casimir Firlit ('57) has been a busy man since St. Rita. After high school, he attended Loyola University (BS) and Loyola Medical School (MD); he interned at Mercy, was a resident at VA Westside, and had a Fellowship at Children's Memorial in Pediatric Urology. His specialty is pediatric kidney transplantation. He was a full professor at Northwestern University for years, and currently is a Professor of Surgery in Urology at Saint Louis University

Joe Scanlon ('58), who was a Converse All-American *selection in basketball and lettered for three years at Marquette University, has been a part of the Chicago area business community ever since graduation. With 40 years experience in the investment business, he has spent the last 25 years with Meisrow Financial. At St. Rita, he had quite a run in basketball; he started 91 straight games and scored 1,025 points before a car accident took him out of the lineup.*

Winners of the 1956 DePaul Christmas Tournament, St. Rita co-captains Frank Smikowski and Mike Maione accepted the first place trophy from Ray Meyer.

Don Petkus was a graduate of the Class of 1958. After St. Rita, Don went to Marquette University (BSME) and then Northwestern University (MBA); on to work in the energy services industry, Don spent over 30 years with Chicago companies Unicom *and* Commonwealth Edison.

St. Rita institutes new program - Science Fair 1956	Fr. Fink ends record 21-year run as Principal 1956	Fr. McLaughlin becomes St. Rita's 6th Rector 1956

1900's 1910's 1920's 1930's 1940's **1950's** 1960's 1970's 1980's 1990's 2000's

St. Rita's automotive shop: l to r, Algis Juodikis ('57) (went on to earn a MSEE at Cal Tech), Mr. Rheinschmidt, and Ray Schaack ('57) (went on to earn a BA at the University of California and played for the Oakland Raiders).

St. Rita always has been an all-boys school - and proudly so, but there are many ways to leave a legacy. Gary Baumgarten ('58), shown above, married and had two daughters - Robin and Holly. Both girls went to Queen of Peace and were St. Rita cheerleaders in the 1980's. Robin now works as a traffic reporter for WGN Channel 9; Holly is the Cheerleader Coach for the St. Rita Cheerleaders, which won the NCA Nationals in 2001/02.

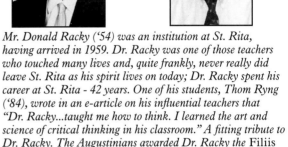

Mr. Donald Racky ('54) was an institution at St. Rita, having arrived in 1959. Dr. Racky was one of those teachers who touched many lives and, quite frankly, never really did leave St. Rita as his spirit lives on today; Dr. Racky spent his career at St. Rita - 42 years. One of his students, Thom Ryng ('84), wrote in an e-article on his influential teachers that "Dr. Racky...taught me how to think. I learned the art and science of critical thinking in his classroom." A fitting tribute to Dr. Racky. The Augustinians awarded Dr. Racky the Filiis Ordinis.

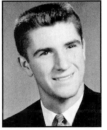

After St. Rita and college at St. Mary's (BA), Dave Eskra ('59) started his business career; focused chiefly in high-tech, Dave was President and CEO of Pansophic Systems (software) for 12 years. He helped take that company public, and then sell it to Computer Associates International. Today Dave is a private investor in technology companies.

Stuart Dybek ('59) attended Loyola in Chicago after St. Rita. Since then, he has become a writer of some note; his work has appeared in The New Yorker, Harper's and Atlantic Monthly, and he has authored five books. His book "The Coast of Chicago" was a selection in the "One Book, One Chicago" reading program put on by Mayor Daley. Stuart teaches creative writing at Western Michigan University. His latest book is "I Sailed with Magellan".

| CCL begins tournament in bowling 1956 | 50th Commencement Exercises 1957 | Enrollment peaks at 2,250 students 1958 |

1900's 1910's 1920's 1930's 1940's 1950's **1960's** 1970's 1980's 1990's 2000's

Graduating Classes

1960 – 536
1961 – 494
1962 – 467
1963 – 354
1964 – 518
1965 – 446
1966 – 456
1967 – 452
1968 – 403
1969 – 380

1960's – Kennedy/Johnson/Nixon ruled the White House, Kennedy the 1st Roman Catholic. Khrushchev and Kennedy had their Cuban Missile Crisis; the Berlin Wall rose up. Vietnam became a war; the TET offensive. The Civil Rights movement was the 1960's. John and Bobby Kennedy, Martin Luther King and Malcolm X assassinated. Man landed on the moon, *Star Trek* on TV; *The Magnificent Seven* and *Psycho* hit the big screen. Chubby Checker released *The Twist*, Bob Dylan his first album; the Beatles arrived, as did Woodstock. Wal-Mart opened. Jack Nicklaus began his run, and Cassius Clay beat Sonny Liston. Pope Paul VI directed the Church (1963-78); John Cody became Chicago's Archbishop (1965-82) and, in time, its 4th Cardinal Priest. Elementary and secondary enrollment in Chicago-area Catholic schools peaked at around 360,000 pupils.

Today they are called 2:07 kids...
Remember When
They were called 2:30 kids?

Remember When the Brothers ran the cafeteria (the Mustang Spa) in the 60's...and hamburgers were 20 cents apiece? L to r, Bros. Martin Shaw, Jerome Sysko, Neil O'Connor, Anthony Schander and Raymond Wallenberg.

Mr. Joseph Bamberger came to St. Rita in 1960, and devoted his whole career to Ritamen. Among his many awards, he holds the distinction of being the first lay person appointed principal of an Augustinian high school - anywhere. The Augustinians honored him with the Filiis Ordinis Award.

St. Rita record
class 536 students
1960

New science
Annex completed
1960

Computer course
offered as elective
1962

1900's 1910's 1920's 1930's 1940's 1950's **1960'S** 1970's 1980's 1990's 2000's

Somebody had to be first, and for St. Rita that young man was McAlister J. Merchant, Jr. ('61). It was an era of civil rights and the opening of new frontiers. In 1957, McAlister enrolled at St. Rita; he would be the first Afro-American graduate of St. Rita four years later in 1961. Since then, McAlister attended the University of Illinois and the Art Center College of Design; he worked for years with the Boy Scouts organization, Microsoft Corporation and now in his own design studio MJM Design, in Ocean Shores, Washington.

Did You Know
Besides being a great baseball player, Jim Olichwier ('62) is lucky - he won the Washington State Lottery

Fr. Richard Allen served at St. Rita in the late-1960's/early-1970's. One of his greatest contributions was his behind-the-scenes efforts helping Principal Fr. Daniel Trusch keep things running after Fr. Trusch suffered a life-threatening accident. Three cheers for Fr. Allen's devotion.

Larry Sullivan ('62) attended De Paul (BA) and Johns Hopkins (MA and PhD) after St. Rita. In a career that has included being Chief of the Rare Book and Special Collections Division at the Library of Congress as well as a Fulbright Scholar in France, Larry now is the Chief Librarian, Associate Dean and a Professor of Criminal Justice at the John Jay College of Criminal Justice of the City University of New York. He is the author or editor of over fifty scholarly books and articles in European and American history, criminology, art history, and other disciplines.

Donnie Mrozek ('65) attended Northwestern (BS), where he lettered in football under Alex Agase, and De Paul (JD) universities after St. Rita. A litigation attorney with over 30 years experience, Don has been admitted to practice before three District Courts and the Seventh Circuit Court of Appeals. He is a Partner and Chairman of Hinshaw & Culbertson, yet still finds time to help out with St. Rita's Valentines Dance.

O.S.A. Brothers Anthony Shander, Jerome Sysko and Daniel Gridley in December, 1966

Father Crawford
becomes St. Rita's
7th Rector 1962

St. Rita football
National
Champion 1963

St. Rita graduates
its 10,000th
student 1963

1900's 1910's 1920's 1930's 1940's 1950's **1960's** 1970's 1980's 1990's 2000's

Father Fink had a custom of celebrating a Brother's Day at St. Rita each year. This 1960's photo captures the assembled in the Garden at the St. Rita Monastery; the Fathers in the first row are, l to r, Seary, Kavanaugh, Fink and Perry.

Did You Know
Kentucky's Coach Adolph Rupp came to St. Rita to watch George Janky play basketball? While scouted, George went to Dayton.

The brothers Hoerster - Ewald (Ed) from the Class of '59 and John from the Class of '67; both are in the St. Rita and Chicago Catholic League Halls of Fame. Ed took his football prowess to Notre Dame, where he lettered for three years; he was drafted in the 10th round by the Bears in the 1963 draft, but chose to play in the Canadian Football League. John went to Northwestern University and, soon thereafter, entered the coaching ranks; he was the Assistant Coach at Gordon Tech for 16 years, until he took the Head Coaching job at Loyola Academy in Wilmette; he took the team to a state championship in 1993; Loyola's football field is named in his honor.

1966/67 Courses of Study
Honors
College Preparatory
General
Data Processing
Industrial Arts

Aeronautics, refrigeration and metal shops were dropped during the 1960's, as student's interests changed; corporations also began preferring their in-house training programs. Automotive shops were dropped in the 1970's.

| Senior Class retreats begin 1966 | Over 1,000 attend summer school 1966 | Midwest OSA celebrates 25 years 1966 |

1900's 1910's 1920's 1930's 1940's 1950's **1960's** 1970's 1980's 1990's 2000's

The Flaherty brothers - all five of them St. Rita graduates: Michael ('69), John ('70), Patrick ('72), Steven ('76) and Thomas ('82). Mike went to Lewis University (BS), where he is in the Athletic Hall of Fame for basketball, and to Chicago State University (MS); today he is a teacher and head basketball coach at Thornridge High School in the south suburbs. John also went to Lewis University (BS), where he is in the Athletic Hall of Fame for wrestling, and to DePaul University (MST) and is a Certified Public Accountant/Certified Financial Planner with his own firm in downtown Chicago. Pat attended Western Illinois University and has worked his way through the ranks to become a Captain in the Chicago Fire Department. Steve attended John Carroll and Illinois State University (BS) and became a Certified Public Accountant with his own practice in downtown Chicago. Tom earned a BS from Northwestern University and today is a broker on the Chicago Mercantile Exchange. Mike played basketball at St. Rita and starred at Lewis University. John played on St. Rita's Chicago Catholic City Championship Lightweight Basketball Team (#34) and was a standout wrestler at Lewis University. Pat played basketball and baseball at St. Rita. Steve played college football at John Carroll. Tom played football at St. Rita and kept on after graduation, playing for Dennis Green at Northwestern University; Tom was then drafted by the Bengals in the NFL draft, and later played for the Bears and Dolphins.

1969 Cascian editors with Moderator Fr. Anthony Hogan; l to r, Mike Kisicki, Larry Bafia, Gary Sladek and James Krukones.

Remember When
Father Francis X. Lawlor, OSA was elected 15th Ward Alderman in late 1960's. He ran for Illinois' 5th Congressional Seat in 1970's. There was just something about the 15th Ward; Ken Jaksy ('52) also was the Alderman at one time.

Remember When
Chicago Police Officer Thomas McKeegan directed traffic at 63rd & Western for over 13 years...surely one of Chicago's finest.

850 young men apply for 1967 admission

Father Trusch becomes St. Rita's 8th Rector 1968

14th Ward football game comes to St. Rita 1969

1900's 1910's 1920's 1930's 1940's 1950's 1960's **1970's** 1980's 1990's 2000's

Graduating Classes

1970 – 459
1971 – 431
1972 – 429
1973 – 347
1974 – 313
1975 – 423
1976 – 422
1977 – 297
1978 – 257
1979 – 230

1970's – The war in Vietnam opened to Cambodia and Laos; Vietnamese cities were bombed. President Nixon ruled, visited the USSR, engineered the Watergate Scandal, and resigned; Jimmy Carter began his only Term, replacing Gerald Ford. The economy suffered wage freezes and oil embargoes, and slid into recession. Northern Ireland erupted; Guyana got Jim Jones; the Shah was driven from Iran. Led Zeppelin and Crosby, Stills, Nash & Young made music; Jimi Hendrix and Janis Joplin never would again. *MASH* hit TV; the *Godfather* hit the big screen. Wozniak and Jobs founded Apple Computer. Three Mile Island had an accident. Business invented junk bonds and leveraged buyouts. Bobby Fischer dominated chess. Two Popes led the Church in 1978 - John Paul I and II: John Paul II was the 265th in line from St. Peter.

Did You Know
The 1970 Prep Bowl game was the last played in Soldier Field before the north end was closed?

Remember Color-Coded Ties
Freshmen – Red
Sophomores – Blue
Juniors – Olive
Seniors - Black

Did You Know
Terry Lein ('76) was St. Rita's 1st National Merit Scholarship finalist – in 1975/76.

L to r, Tom Byrne, Tim Maher, Mike Georgopolis, Dennis Bartz, Brother Jerome, John Rock, Tom Schumacher, Ed Gronkowski, and Greg Cozzi. Ever wonder what they're doing today: Tom is in sales and transportation for a beer distributor, Tim runs a Sports Outlet, Mike is a broker/trader, Dennis is a dentist, Brother Jerome is still at St. Rita, John was last heard to be in Colorado, Tom manages a message service center, Ed works for the Public Building Commission, and Greg helped sell his family's scrap iron business after running it for a number of years.

St. Rita returns focus to college preparatory 1970

St. Rita football takes Chicago Prep Bowl 1970

Father Flach becomes St. Rita's 9th Rector 1971

1900's 1910's 1920's 1930's 1940's 1950's 1960's **1970's** 1980's 1990's 2000's

Ernie Mrozek ('71) left St. Rita and attended the University of Illinois. He lives in Memphis, but maintains a strong presence in Chicago. Ernie is President and CFO of The Service-Master Company, a FORTUNE 500 firm. Ernie has been active on the Pat Cronin Golf Outing Committee since the start.

Ray Jagielski ('71) has been a Ritaman on many fronts. After high school, Ray went to Wabash College (BA) in Crawfordsville, Indiana and John Marshall Law School (JD). Today, Ray Jagieliski is Judge Jageliski; he serves as a Circuit Court Judge in the Cook County system, County Division. Ray found enough time between graduation and judicial appointment to be a part of St. Rita's football coaching staff; he was on the staff during the 1978 State Championship season.

Did You Know
Rich Urbanski ('69), Tim Maher ('71) and Brian Panick ('75) have been elected to the 16" Softball Hall of Fame?

Marge Byrne married into the St. Rita family and never left. After marrying Tom ('45), they had four sons: Tom ('72), Dan ('74), Terry ('76) and Jim ('79). Marge started working in the office in 1977/78 and remains there today. Next up, the third generation of the Byrne family.

Basketball has always been big at St. Rita. Here, John Bonk ('75) gives it up for the team. John Bonk returned to St. Rita and is the Athletic Director.

Fr. Richard McGrath came to St. Rita in 1973 and taught for a number of years. He currently heads up Providence High School in New Lenox.

St. Rita did not have a female teacher until 1975; meet Ms. Sue Whooley (now Mrs. Sue Ksystof) still teaching Chemistry 30 years later. The student looking in is Stan Kastelic ('78), who came back and is a teacher at St. Rita.

Did You Know
The Catholic League adopted OT for football in the early 1970's, making the scoreless tie between St. Rita and St. Laurence on 9/27/70 the last in CCL play.

St. Rita football takes Chicago Prep Bowl 1971	St. Rita starts its 1st Pride Week 1974/75	Chicago Catholic League joins I.H.S.A. 1975

1900's 1910's 1920's 1930's 1940's 1950's 1960's **1970's** 1980's 1990's 2000's

1975 varsity football coaching staff: l to r, Pat Cronin, Tom Sola, John Buckley, Bob Craig, Bill Brady, Tom Berry and John Pergi

ST. RITA HIGH SCHOOL
BINGO
EVERY THURS. 7³⁰ P.M.
OVER $1600. In PRIZES
20-GAMES - $40. $100. $125. $150. $175. $500.

Remember when Messrs. Grill, Brodnicki and Dvorak started the weekly bingo games in the gym as a fundraiser for St. Rita?

These four pictures, clockwise from upper left: while trolleys were gone, getting to school didn't change that much; seniors took over for the Rita Rooters and named themselves ZORK; technology before the PC - mainframes and IBM punch cards; and catching hall duty never was the worst duty and you could earn one quarter credit.

| St. Rita hockey takes Kennedy Cup 1975 | St. Rita restarts 8th grade open houses 1976 | St. Rita starts busing program 1977 |

1900's 1910's 1920's 1930's 1940's 1950's 1960's **1970'S** 1980's 1990's 2000's

Fred Richardson, Jr. graduated from St. Rita in 1978. After St. Rita and college, Fred enrolled in medical school at Rush Medical College. He received his M.D. degree and established a practice in Family Medicine, in which he is Board Certified. With admitting privileges at Rush University Medical Center (which includes the old Presbyterian-St. Luke's hospital), he has offices in Oak Park. His legacy continues through his son, a member of the Class of 2007.

TV's Johnny Morris and Coach Cronin entertain the Rita Cheerleaders.

During the championship 1978/79 season with a 5–0 start, football was such a draw that Homecoming had to be moved to Soldier Field; the 1st high school homecoming on the Lakefront drew 15,000 and St. Rita beat St. Laurence 14 to 6

It was a time when A-V didn't mean VHS or CD's or DVD's; here John Kramer ('79) brings Mr. Dvorak a film for Physics class.

St. Rita celebrated its 75th Anniversary in style - with guest host Bob Hope. In the picture are, l to r, Fr. John Flynn ('45) (whose father Clarence was from the Class of 1915), Bob Hope, and Fr. David Brecht. Bob Hope was MC at the celebration held at the Auditorium Theatre on November 11, 1979 - 75 years and counting.

| St. Rita football takes Chicago Prep Bowl 1977 | St. Rita state football champion 1978 | Father Brecht becomes St. Rita's 10th Rector 1979 |

1900's 1910's 1920's 1930's 1940's 1950's 1960's 1970's **1980's** 1990's 2000's

Graduating Classes

1980 – 226
1981 – 254
1982 – 287
1983 – 335
1984 – 349
1985 – 348
1986 – 285
1987 – 305
1988 – 261
1989 – 264

1980's – Mt. St. Helens erupted, as did battles in far away places: the Falklands, Grenada and Panama. Ronald Reagan unseated Jimmy Carter; George H. Bush would be next in line. Iran's Ayatollah released American hostages after 444 days. Lech Walesa rose in a Polish shipyard strike. Pink Floyd, Madonna and Michael Jackson made music; John Lennon couldn't anymore. *ET* went to the movies, *Cheers* to TV. The economy rose out of the recession. The space shuttle *Challenger* exploded. The first heart transplant took place, cell phones debuted, and the personal computer arrived on desktops. Chicago welcomed its 5th man who would become Cardinal Priest – Joseph Bernardin (1982-96).

1980/81 Coaching Staff; l to r, Tom Nall, Dan Capron, Mike Kisicki, Mike Moysis, Frank Paduch, Pat Cronin, Jim Misiora, Jim Segredo and Norb Lasky.

St. Rita celebrates
75th Anniversary
1980

St. Rita begins
Hall of Fame
1980

St. Rita wins state
AAA ice hockey
1982

1900's 1910's 1920's 1930's 1940's 1950's 1960's 1970's **1980's** 1990's 2000's

Did You Know
The football coaching staff prepared for big games by watching 8mm and 16mm game films projected on a bed sheet tacked to Coach Cronin's wall. Films were taken by Tony Golczak ('70).

The old trophy hall gets the 1981/82 State trophy in AAA Hockey. Top row, l to r, AD Jim Segredo ('73), Bob Valentine ('82), Head Coach Jim Misiora ('67); bottom, l to r, Dave Cronin ('82), Jeff Bollman ('84), Al Bromowicz ('82) and Matt McCurie ('82).

Coaches, Assistants, Trainers and Managers, 1982 football had it all. Above, l to r, Bill Brady, Jerry Monte, Jim Angsten, Pat Cronin, Ray Jagielski, Ray Bugal and Jim Prunty; below, l to r, Dennis Krokos, John Clemmons, Mark Klein, Kevin O'Hara, Joe Lacny, George Baker and, bottom, Ball Retreiver Glenn.

| 75th Commencement Exercises 1982 | Father Murphy becomes St. Rita's 11th Rector 1983 | St. Rita Board of Advisors created 1984 |

1900's 1910's 1920's 1930's 1940's 1950's 1960's 1970's **1980's** 1990's 2000's

Ron Bedore, Rich Baran, Brian Sheedy (all '85): Seniors, CCHL All-Stars and Forwards

Did You Know

DePaul's Coach Joey Meyer and Notre Dame's Digger Phelps both came to St. Rita to watch Curtis Price play basketball? Curtis started for three years at DePaul.

Jim Segredo ('73) long part of the heart and soul of St. Rita. In 20 years between 1977 and 1997 this Ritaman served as Teacher, Coach, Athletic Director and Vice President, including a stint as Director of Development. He currently is President of Montini High School in Lombard.

And who could forget Mr. "E"...Mr. James Economakas. Mr. "E" started at St. Rita in 1952 and retired in 1984. Here he is shown with one of the thousands of students whose lives he touched.

Fr. Roland Follmann, Prior and Dean of Guidance.

Mass on the football field in the 1980's: Fathers Pazera, Murphy, Follmann, Brecht, Turcich and Van Overbeek.

St. Rita football field renamed *Pat Cronin Field* 1984

St. Rita hockey takes Kennedy Cup 1984

St. Rita basketball Thanksgiving event starts 1986

1900's 1910's 1920's 1930's 1940's 1950's 1960's 1970's **1980's** 1990's 2000's

1986 14th Ward Football Day - St. Rita vs Mt. Carmel; l to r, Judge John McGury, long-time Chicago City Clerk Walter Kozubowski ('57), 14th Ward Alderman Edward Burke, and principals Frs. Patrick Murphy, O.S.A. ('66) and Bob Carroll, O. Carm..

Remember When
St. Rita used Marquette Park as its home field in baseball, never played a home game because of the wet fields, and still won the CCL title.

Mike Kisicki ('69) plays Ed McMahon to St. Rita's Karnak - Jim Misiora ('67).

Remember When
The baseball team would travel to Louisville at Spring Break to get in some extra games?

Brother Mike Schweifler, now Father Mike Schweifler. As a young teacher at St. Rita in the 1980's, he was affectionately referred to as GI Bro.

Remember When
Seniors could leave the campus during lunch periods

| US Department of Education honors St. Rita 1987 | St. Rita institutes Kairos Retreats 1989 | Father Danber becomes St. Rita's 12th Rector 1989 |

1900's 1910's 1920's 1930's 1940's 1950's 1960's 1970's 1980's **1990'S** 2000's

Graduating Classes

1990 – 251
1991 – 221
1992 – 205
1993 – 214
1994 – 164
1995 – 253
1996 – 193
1997 – 168
1998 – 174
1999 – 140

1990's – The 21st U.S. Census showed population exceeding 250 million. The Persian Gulf War was waged; the USSR dismantled. Serbia, Bosnia and Croatia ended fighting. Bill Clinton's star rose. Riots erupted in Los Angeles in response to Rodney King; Branch Davidians were exposed in Waco, Texas. The Internet arrived, cloning embryos began and everyone prepared for Y2K. The Chicago Bulls took home a six-pack; Tiger Woods rose. The Murrah Federal Building in Oklahoma City was brought down, showing problems close to home. *Titanic*, *Schindler's List* and *Forrest Gump* were on the big screen. Chicago's native son became its 8th Archbishop (1996) and 6th Cardinal Priest, Francis George, OMI.

It was during Fr. Bernard Danber's watch that St. Rita moved its campus from 63rd Street to 77th Street. Here Fr. Danber enrolls another in the long line of Mustangs, this time Bishop Wilton Gregory; St. Rita and the Bishop go back a way: it was Bishop Gregory who ordained Fr. Danber, Fr. Wes Benak and Fr. Tom McCarthy.

What would happen if we had a St. Rita walk-a-thon and no one checked in?

Fraternal twins Mike and Frank Kelly, both of the Class of 1992.

St. Rita moves to
Quigley South
1990

Football stadium
erected on new
campus 1990

Midwest OSA
celebrates 50
years 1991

Did You Know
Parts of the 1993 movie RUDY (the practice at Joliet Catholic) were filmed in St. Rita's football stadium?

At top are the Thirteen Blind Mice, *with Dr. K and Bro. Jack bringing up the rear; the picture dates to May 16, 1992 at the Senior Prom held in the Grand Ballroom of the* Chicago Hilton. *Below is a picture of John Chico helping Fr. O'Connor enroll a new Mustang - in this case, Fr. Miguel Orcasitas, Prior General of the Order of St. Augustine. At right is proof positive that the 90's affected everyone; he may be a Mustang now, but where did you say Mr. Standring went to high school?*

St. Rita has its 1ˢᵗ Mother/Son dance 1991/92

St. Rita adds all-weather track to FB field 1991

St. Rita hockey takes Kennedy Cup 1992

1900's 1910's 1920's 1930's 1940's 1950's 1960's 1970's 1980's **1990's** 2000's

Clockwise from upper left: While they look like the Village People, *St. Rita students prove they know how to have fun at one of the many events held during the school year; this particular picture dates to 1994/95.* Rocky-the-Rita-Rot *was a part of many activities during the 1990's, especially accompanying the outdoor clubs. The 1994/95 Homecoming Queen and her Court: Adolfo Viezca with Erin McKinney, Vinny Lopez with Mandie McClenan, Kevin Gade with Queen Ann Early, Aaron Malnarick with Tanya Beaumier, Kevin Prunty with Jenny Spaeth and Eric Chico with Gina Calderone. Brave young* Ritamen *working their way down the Fashion Show aisle; no, their get-up was not suggested for a new dress code.*

St. Rita 63rd Street
Monastery closes
1993

Father O'Connor
becomes St. Rita's
1st President 1993

Mr. Bamberger
13th Principal at
St. Rita 1993

1900's 1910's 1920's 1930's 1940's 1950's 1960's 1970's 1980's **1990's** 2000's

The 1990's were a period of change and transition at St. Rita: above shows the interview process for new leadership; at middle is the new transportation system put in effect to draw students from the suburbs; and at bottom is the new nautical course added to the Technical School. Seriously though, St. Rita is lucky to have leaders such as Don Racky, Joe Bamberger and Fr. Tom McCarthy - men who know how to play hard and work hard; the large campus parking lot, allowed students to drive and park safely; and the Anita Dee II was the site of a number of Junior Proms through the 90's.

1st four-year graduates on new campus 1994

St. Rita's *Cronin Field* gets stadium lights 1999

US News & World Report honors St. Rita 1999

1900's 1910's 1920's 1930's 1940's 1950's 1960's 1970's 1980's 1990's **2000's**

Graduating Classes

2000 – 124
2001 – 192
2002 – 210
2003 – 177
2004 – 176

2000's – The Taliban in Afghanistan became a touchstone. Osama Bin Laden, al Qaeda and Saddam Hussein became epithets. The space shuttle *Columbia* disintegrated on re-entry. North Korea rattled its nuclear saber. George W. Bush squeaked into the White House. Milosevic was charged in The Hague. Terrorists brought down the World Trade Center towers. Enron and WorldCom engendered corporate scandals. Enrollment in the 283 Chicago-area Catholic schools, both elementary and secondary, settled around 110,000.

We have Coach Nee, they have Bryant Jones...you do the math!

These three photos, from left: Chemistry opens a lot of eyes; Fr. Tom travels to Israel; and Fr. McNicholas is the grand old master in Counseling

Father McCarthy
2nd President
2000

100th Anniversary
of Canonization
St. Rita 2000

Father McCarthy
14th Principal
2002

1900's 1910's 1920's 1930's 1940's 1950's 1960's 1970's 1980's 1990's **2000's**

One Sutdent to the Other
Why can't we wear "hoodies"?
All the Augustinians do!

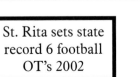
St. Rita sets state
record 6 football
OT's 2002

St. Rita state
wrestling champ
2003 + 2004

St. Rita celebrates
100th Anniversary
2005

ATHLETICS AT ST. RITA

Talk to any school administration and they'll agree that athletics are a big part in the development of the whole student; this is true at St. Rita, and has been ever since it fielded its first football team in 1908. But how does one compare teams from year-to-year, or decade-to-decade? You don't. You don't because the organization of teams from any era changes vis-à-vis another era. Conference alignments adjust regularly, as do the requirements for admission. For example, in the old days, basketball teams were fielded on the basis of height: called *Juniors or Lights* (under 5'8") and *Seniors or Heavies* (over 5'8" in height); and those were just the varsity upperclassmen, the lower level freshman and sophomore teams being called *Bantams* and *Flys*. Today, we divide by varsity and the junior levels (for example, junior varsity), with no regard to a player's particular vertical challenge. Almost every time a team is added or dropped from a conference, alignments change. Throughout, balance is the goal.

If you go back to St. Rita's founding, there was a Cook County League loosely representing most of the schools in the greater Chicagoland area, Catholic and public; teams made arrangements with individual teams, and there wasn't much formal organization. In 1912, the Chicago Catholic League was formed to organize the Catholic schools into competitive groups. Shortly thereafter, a new Chicago Public League superseded the Cook County League, with suburban schools looking for their own conference arrangements in a new Suburban League. But, even with this more formal arrangement, schools were not forced to remain in a particular alignment.

If a team felt it could be accorded better treatment in another conference, it might change allegiances. Also, if you carried enough weight, you could form your own conference. For example, in 1961 the four Christian Brother schools – St. George, St. Patrick, St. Mel and De LaSalle – withdrew from the Catholic League and formed their own...the Chicagoland Prep League. While this alignment didn't survive, it does show why comparing one era to another is impossible. Another example is found when Catholic schools participate in public conferences, such as some Catholic ice hockey programs playing in public conferences, to gain different competition or additional games; in fact, some schools may participate in both Catholic and public conferences at the same time. Change is the only constant in athletics.

That said, St. Rita has enjoyed a stellar history in sports over the last one hundred years, with numerous national, state, city and conference championships in a variety of sports. Through the years, particular sports have been added and dropped, and sometimes reinstated, as conditions and the interests of the student body change. At present, St. Rita offers competitive level opportunities in baseball, basketball, bowling, cross country, football, golf, gymnastics, ice hockey, soccer, swimming, track, volleyball, water polo and wrestling; and these are just the competitive teams. Lineups also are fielded as club teams or intramural squads, and that doesn't even touch on the 30-some activities offered at St. Rita, some state sponsored.

While some of the greatest rivalries and traditions remain within the Chicago Catholic League (for example, the Kennedy Cup), one could never discount those between the Catholic and the Public leagues (for example, the Chicago Prep Bowl); with more organizational control of high school sports exerted by the Illinois High School Association over the last 30 years, contests between upstate teams and downstate teams now are a regular occurrence (for example, the State Championships). Through it all, St. Rita has been a major participant and a major contributor.

BASEBALL

Baseball has been the sport of choice for almost as long as St. Rita has been in existence. When the equipment was still at a rudimentary stage, St. Rita was fielding teams in the various Chicago area conferences: such as, the Chicago Youth Organization (CYO teams), the Chicago Amateur Baseball League (CABL teams), Chicago Catholic League (CCL teams) and a host of other conference alignments over the years. St. Rita won CCL titles in 1922, 1923, 1929 and 1930; sectional titles in 1928, 1929 and 1930. In the CABL starting in the 1940's, St. Rita took six championships in ten years.

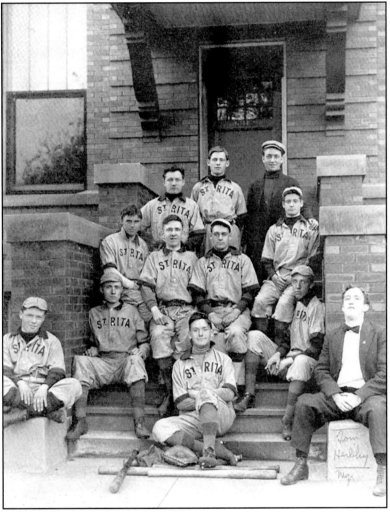

St. Rita baseball, circa 1911. Tom Herlihy, Manager in bow tie.

On a statewide basis, high school games are traced back to 1884 in Illinois. The first state championship tournament was held in 1940 as an invitational; two years later the I.H.S.A. began sponsoring the state championship, all games on the standard of nine innings. In 1954, high school competition was standardized on a seven-inning format; teams were split across two classes, A and AA, in 1978. St. Rita always has been competitive in baseball, and most recent history shows eight regional championships for the school: 1986, 1991, 1994, 1996, 1997, 2002, 2003 and 2004. In the most recent season, 652 teams competed in the state series. Through the years, St. Rita has prepared a number of baseball players for the college and professional scene.

Nick Etten ('31)

Ed Farmer ('67)

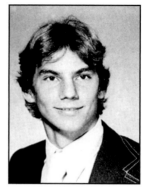

Jim Clancy ('74)

Over the years, St. Rita has sent a number of athletes on to successful college careers and/or the Pro's; three such Ritamen are Nick Etten, Ed Farmer and Jim Clancy. Nicholas Raymond Thomas Etten played nine seasons in the Pro's, always at 1st base - two years with Connie Mack's Philadelphia Athletics, three with the crosstown Phillies and four with Joe McCarthy's New York Yankees; Nick earned a World Series ring in 1943, was a 1945 Yankee All-Star and batted .277 lifetime. Edward Joseph Farmer spent 11 seasons in the majors, eight in the American League; Ed was drafted by the Cleveland Indians in the 5th round of the 1967 amateur draft; used chiefly as a closer, he appeared in 370 games; credited with 30 saves in 1980, Ed represented the Chicago White Sox in the 1980 All-Star game. James Clancy was drafted by the Texas Rangers in the 4th round of the 1974 amateur draft; traded to Toronto two years later in the expansion draft, he played 12 years in Canada and three more in Houston; chiefly a starting pitcher he appeared in 472 games, winning 140; Jim was a Toronto All-Star in 1982.

When it comes to coaching, two of the greats in St. Rita baseball are Fr. J.J. O'Malley (left) and Joe Porrevecchio.

St. Rita won Chicago Catholic League titles in 1922, 23, 27, 28, 29, 30, 31, 49, 60, 65, 72, 76, 81, 82, 84, 86, 87, 88, 89, 93, 95, 01 and 04; Chicago Amateur Baseball League (CABL) titles in 1947, 48, 49, 50, 52 and 53; I.H.S.A. District titles in 1977; I.H.S.A. Regional titles in 1986, 91, 94, 96, 97, 02, 03 and 04.

St. Rita kids always could play baseball; their numerous CCL and CABL titles through the 1920's and 1930's are proof. Shown above is one of those 1920's teams, coached as usual by Fr. Jackie Harris. At right is a picture of the 1929 Championship team; this team won the Chicago Catholic League title.

St. Rita fields competitive teams at the junior varsity and varsity level; in some years, so many students came out for baseball that more than one team would be fielded at each level. Baseball always has been a popular high school sport, even more so because one doesn't need a lot of specialized equipment to play.

1976/77 District Winner

1985/86 Regional Winner

1990/91 Regional Winner

1993/94 Regional Winner

1995/96 Regional Winner

1996/97 Regional Winner

2001/02 Regional Winner

2002/03 Regional Winner

St. Rita's 2003/04 Baseball team that went to state...above in the pre-game line-up at Elfstrom Stadium in Geneva and, below, in a team picture. As the first and only St. Rita baseball team to reach the Illinois Elite-8, it has a lot of which to be proud. This Team could hit, as it's .394 team batting average proved; as a Team they stroked 428 hits during the season with 324 runs batted in - both Top-25 records in Illinois since the I.H.S.A. began keeping statistics.

Between coaches Jim Prunty and Mike Zunica, they can account for all but one regional championship for St. Rita. Jim Prunty (left), a five-time *Tony Lawless Award* winner, was Head Coach of the team between 1986/87 and 1995/96 and had a record of 261-95-2. Mike Zunica (right) has coached the team for the last eight years and holds a St. Rita record of 215-90-0; he has the distinction of coaching the latest team that won regional, sectional and super-sectional titles on their way to the Illinois Elite-8. These two coaches share almost 500 St. Rita victories.

BASKETBALL

St. Rita has fielded basketball teams since the 1920's, almost as long as the football programs. In the early days, besides conference contests in basketball, national tournaments and championships were held each year to provide the best competition for teams…but the Catholic schools were not allowed in these games. In response, some Chicago-area Catholic schools and prominent sportswriters cobbled together a national basketball tournament for Catholic schools. The first tournament was held in 1924 and national champions were crowned through 1941; World War II and eventual détente between the Catholic and Public leagues brought this national event to an end. In the 18 years this tournament was held, Chicago-area Catholic schools won the trophy ten times: St. Mel in 1925, Joliet De LaSalle in 1927/28/34, Chicago De LaSalle in 1929/30/36, St. Patrick's in 1932, Fenwick in 1937, and Leo in 1941.

On a state basis back in the old days, the Catholic league crowned its own champion in the Chicago area each year…the *de facto* Catholic state champion; while a broader tournament was attempted between 1929 and 1941, it never caught on and was dropped in 1941, when private schools first were permitted to join the I.H.S.A.. While area Catholic teams went their own way for a long time, the entire Chicago Catholic League entered the state tournament in 1975, three years after the tournament was split into small and large schools, A and AA; in the recent season, 716 teams competed in the state series. While St. Rita has not won a state championship, it has accounted itself well over the years in Catholic League and City play; St. Rita won the City Championship defeating the Roosevelt *Rough Riders* 69-58 in 1952 under coach Barney Badke; the 1970 Light Team under Coach Bob Kopecky won the All-Chicago Catholic League title, defeating Loyola.

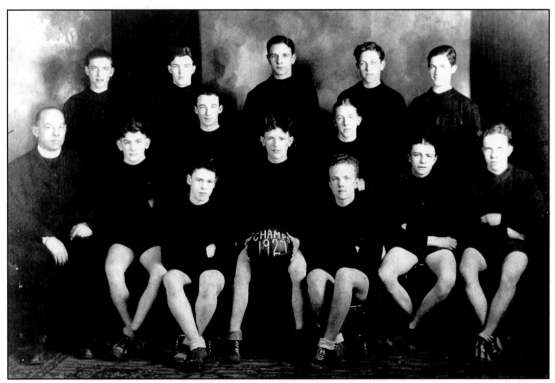

With Father Jackie Harris Coaching/Moderating yet another sport, the 1927 basketball squad played very well. Those identified in the picture were, l to r: top row far left, Ed Murney and next to last on right, Bill Mulvihill; middle row, Fr. Harris, Jim Connelly, Howie Meade, Tony Hetart, Jim Bookley, Wally Knapp and unidentified; bottom row was, Noonan and Bill Parks.

*Head Varsity Basketball Coach
Barney Badke was a 1935 graduate
of St. Rita.*

*Coach Barney Badke's 1952 Senior Varsity basketball team was a winner. In 1943
Chicago began an intra-city basketball championship at the end of the season; this match
up of the Catholic league and the Public league champion was patterned after football's
Chicago Prep Bowl that began nine years earlier. St. Rita's exploits in basketball
really turned around in 1950, when the varsity team won the Chicago Catholic League
championship...St. Rita's first in basketball; two years later in 1952 St. Rita's team took
the Chicago Catholic League title and added the City championship to its laurels..another
St. Rita first in basketball. In the title match against Roosevelt at Chicago Stadium on
April 4, 1952, St. Rita center Ken Jaksy scored 40 points.*

History of State Playoffs

1909 1ˢᵗ state championship
   held, district winners to
   the finals.

1922 Sectional level of
   play added to state
   tournament.

1928 Chicago Public League
   teams enter state play

1936 Regional level of
   play added to state
   tournament

1941 Private teams allowed in
   state tournament

1975 Chicago Catholic League
   teams enter state play

*The 1970 Lights basketball team won the Chicago Catholic League title; the team
defeated sister-school Mendel to lock up the South Section CCL championship,
and beat Gordon Tech and Loyola in the Catholic City match.*

*At right, 1947/48 St. Rita
Champion Bantamweights.*

John Egan ('60) was a St. Rita basketball star (Mr. Mustang as a senior) who found even greater glory in the college ranks. Off to Loyola-Chicago, he played on the 1963 NCAA Championship team; in the final against Cincinnati, the starting five (Hunter, Harkness, Rouse, Miller and Egan) played the game plus one overtime without substitutes. John is a criminal defense attorney.

Curtis Price ('88) was one of the best in St. Rita basketball, of any period. Digger Phelps from Notre Dame and Joey Meyer from De Paul came to St. Rita to watch him play. Curtis, a 4-year varsity player at St. Rita, went to De Paul where he was a starter for three years. Broken wrists and a blown ACL kept him from advancing to the pros. Curtis works on the Board of Trade.

McGovern Classic Winners

1987/88	**St. Rita**
1988/89	Eisenhower
1989/90	Eisenhower
1990/91	Shepard
1991/92	Hillcrest
1992/93	**St. Rita**
1993/94	Brother Rice
1994/95	Brother Rice
1995/96	Bloom
1996/97	Bloom
1997/98	Hillcrest
1998/99	Brother Rice
1999/00	**St. Rita**
2000/01	Homewood-Flossmoor
2001/02	**St. Rita**
2002/03	Hales Franciscan
2003/04	Homewood-Flossmoor
2004/05	Homewood-Flossmoor

Originally St. Rita's Thanksgiving Classic, this tournament was renamed in honor of Mr. Tom McGovern, who coached at St. Rita for a number of years; the tournament was renamed in 1991. Today, the McGovern Classic is one of the premier holiday basketball tournaments.

Let's just call this the Team That Time Forgot. *The Varsity basketball team in the 1993/94 school year was pretty successful; the Team finished 2nd in the Chicago Catholic League, and that was against some particularly tough competition. But, sometimes fame and fortune follow. Six months after the basketball season closed, the 1ˢᵗ place team from St. Martin de Porres was disqualified for using ineligible players; St. Rita basketball advanced to a 1ˢᵗ place finish in the Chicago Catholic League. Since the final results were not in until the Summer of 1994, these players never received the recognition they were due. The photo at right honors their accomplishment.*

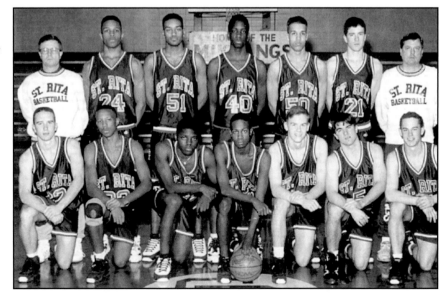

Besides City championships, St. Rita has won numerous Catholic League championships (1950, 52, 53, 63, 65, 66, 70 and 03 tournaments), and earned berths in three regionals of the state playoffs: 1981/82, 1999/00 and 2002/03. In the 2002/2003 season, St. Rita had three Division I recruits on its team: Mike Rembert, Rashay Russell and Jerrah Young, all graduates of 2003.

Michael Rembert ('03) was a Division I recruit of Bradley University.

Rashay Russell ('03) was a Division I recruit of the University of Toledo.

Jerrah Young ('03) was a Division I recruit of West Virginia University.

1999/00 I.H.S.A. Basketball Regional Champions; Record 19 - 9; Head Coach John Bonk.

Head Coach John Bonk ('75).

2002/03 I.H.S.A. Basketball Regional Champions; Chicago Catholic League South Champions; Record 20 - 9; Head Coach John Bonk.

BOWLING

While girl's bowling has been conducted as varsity level interscholastic competition since 1944, and sponsored by the I.H.S.A. in a state championship series since 1973, it is a relatively new varsity offering for boys in the state, even though men's bowling leagues dominate the local lanes. Bowling has been a sport for St. Rita men for years, the first team fielded in 1939/40; coached by Fr. Ralph Giovinetti, St. Rita won the 1971 City Championship; St. Rita bowlers also won championships in 1985/86 and 1991/92. It wasn't until 2002/03 that boys bowling was initiated as a competitive sport at the I.H.S.A. level, at which time St. Rita joined; it is conducted as a winter activity and is directed by Coach Katie Curran. St. Rita offers both junior varsity and varsity levels of play, and competes in the Chicago Catholic League; St. Rita keglers can earn a berth in the state tournament series. In their first season of play, one individual qualified for State (Matt McCarthy). In their second season (2003/04), the Team qualified; St. Rita made it to the final 24 teams (out of 124) in state competition and finished 20th in the State.

While no team picture of the 1971 City Championship Team remains, a number of players were identified. At top left, Ken Gronski, Mike O'Connor and Ken Sobkowiak applaud someone's roll; at right, Dan Tracey takes aim. The 1971 team finished CCL competition at 8-1-1, the two 1's to Brother Rice.

Fr. Ralph Giovinetti.

Mrs. Katie Curran

Matt McCarthy qualified for State (St. Rita's first) in 2002/03 as an individual, and finished 55th overall. He rolled a 1,848 for nine games over two days.

1982 Chicago Catholic League Champions

CROSS COUNTRY

It is thought that the first cross country competition between high schools dates to 1908 in a Cook County League open meet. In 1946, the I.H.S.A. sponsored the first state championships in cross country; in 1976 competitive cross country was split along two classes, A and AA. In the most recent season, 457 teams competed in the state series. Founded in 1958 by Fr. John Burkhart, St. Rita has participated in cross country for many years, sometimes with enough students to fill out a team and sometimes only with particularly gifted individual performers. For example, St. Rita's team earned its first I.H.S.A. District win in 1979; in 1982, John Herlihy ('83) competed as an individual for St. Rita; John finished a respectable 20th (14:54) in state level competition that year, and went on to even greater glory at the college level. St. Rita won a pair of state district meets under Coach Mike Kisicki in 1978/79 and 1979/80. In the 1990/91 season, St. Rita won its first-ever Chicago Catholic League title and earned a berth in the state series by advancing through the qualifier; Coach Mike Murphy directed the team that season.

*The 1978/79 Cross Country team (above) was the first at St. Rita to win an I.H.S.A. District Title; the team was coached by Mike Kisicki and captained by Cuthberto Viramontes, Dan Cullinan, Frank Sheeran and Bob Diamond. The dog in the picture was a stray picked up by the Team and named **Districts**; Coach Kisicki kept the dog for the next nine years.*

The 1979/80 team also would win the District title. The 1980/81 team would just miss at Districts, but would be the third consecutive team to qualify for the regional playoffs in the State tournament; the picture at right shows the State Team.

John Herlihy ('83)

St. Rita runners Bob Wolak and Roy Bricker run along Marquette Park lagoon. Roy would set the St. Rita mark of 15:04 for the 3-mile run during the 1974/75 school year; John Herlihy would beat it during 1982/83 with a 14:54.

After St. Rita, John Herlihy ('83) ran both track and cross-country at Benedictine University and competed in the cross-country nationals in 1986. He has degrees from Benedictine and IIT-Chicago. He is shown at graduation (top), and today.

Mike Kisicki ('69) came to St. Rita in 1973 and has spent all but two of the years since then forming Ritamen; with stints as Athletic Director, Head Disciplinarian and Assistant Principal, he also found time to moderate and coach a number of activities and sports over the years. One of those was as Head Coach of the Cross Country team; in 1979 in only his fourth year at the helm, the team won its first District Meet. St. Rita runners won more than two dozen individual trophies under Coach Kisicki.

First year Head Coach Mike Murphy led the St. Rita team to its first Chicago Catholic League title in 1990/91, and to Peoria for the State tournament, the first time as a team. Coach Murphy was a highly regarded coach and teacher, and was the only hold-over from the Quigley South coaching fraternity.

The 1990/91 Chicago Catholic League Championship team. Top to bottom, l to r, Head Coach Mike Murphy, K. Foucher, G. Armour, A. Buttimer, and Coach Art Kimber; M. Gill, R. Schuch, R. Ralphson and R. Herrera; S. Keller and F. Gill.

Chris Kozubowski ('95) became the first St. Rita runner to win the CCL individual Cross Country championship; he set the record at Montrose Harbor during the 1993/94 school year.

Football

St. Rita has had a storied football program. Ever since it fielded its first team in 1908, St. Rita has been synonymous with excellence in football. Whether it was the City champion in 1923, or the four Prep Bowl championships that followed; St. Rita football enjoyed national ranking for a number of years, culminating as the consensus national champion by the Associated Press in 1963. The history of St. Rita football pre-dates the modern football field dimensions; before 1912, football fields were 110 yards long.

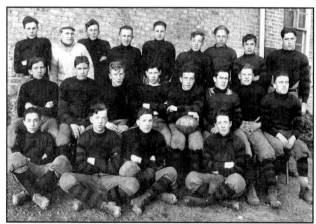

These pictures illustrate the earliest football teams at St. Rita. At upper left is a picture of the 1910 or 1911 football team, posed as usual on the steps on the Oakley side of the original building; note the leather helmets held by the boys in the lower right; Father J.J. Barthouski was the Coach, and this team went 8 and 3 during the season. At upper right is the 1911 or 1912 football team; note in both pictures Tom Herlihy as Manager, just like he was in baseball. At left is the 1914 football team. At bottom left is the 1920 squad, Fr. Jackie Harris is shown at lower right in the picture. Directly below is a picture that is believed to show the City Championship team from 1923; this team went on to beat McBride High School in St. Louis to win a mythical Midwest Title.

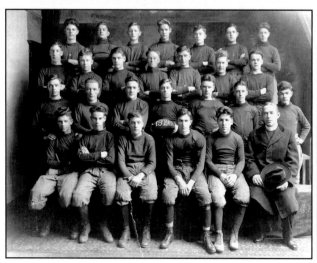

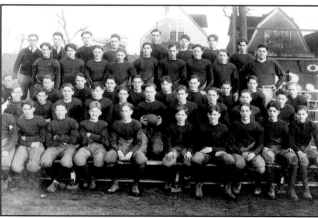

After the 1923 City championship in football, the program ran into a quiet period. All the while, St. Rita kept developing the skills and talent to emerge at the forefront in time. During this period, football grew tremendously, from the invention of the forward pass by Knute Rockne to the specialization of offensive and defensive positions. Equipment changed, leather helmets giving way to safer protective gear.

The year 1934 was one of the lowest periods of the Great Depression. Yet Chicago began many new initiatives, in spite of the economic circumstances, and sports were a big part of the innovations. In Chicago, the first College All-Star game was played against the Chicago Bears (tie); the Chicago Blackhawks won their first Stanley Cup; Chicago would host its second World's Fair – the Century of Progress Exposition – for the second summer; and Chicago Mayor Edward Kelly began a fundraiser for area children around Thanksgiving, pitting the Public League champion against the Catholic League champion in a football match at Soldiers Field - and the Chicago Prep Bowl was born.

CHICAGO PREP BOWL
PUBLIC LEAGUE CITY CHAMPION VERSUS CATHOLIC LEAGUE CITY CHAMPION
CATHOLIC LEAGUE LEADS SERIES 47 - 22 – 2

1934 Lindblom beat Leo
1935 Lindblom beat Leo
1936 Austin tied Fenwick
1937 Austin beat Leo 26 to 0 in front of estimated 110,000 on 11/27/37
1938 Fenger beat Mt. Carmel
1939 Fenger tied Mt. Carmel

1940 Fenger beat Leo
1941 Leo beat Tilden
1942 Leo beat Tilden
1943 St. George beat Phillips
1944 Tilden beat Weber
1945 Fenwick beat Tilden
1946 Fenger beat Weber
1947 Austin beat Leo
1948 Lindblom beat Fenwick
1949 Schurz beat Fenwick

1950 Mt. Carmel beat Lane
1951 Mt. Carmel beat Lindblom
1952 Mt. Carmel beat Austin
1953 St. George beat Austin
1954 Fenger beat Mt. Carmel
1955 Vocational beat Weber
1956 Leo beat Calumet
1957 Mendel beat Calumet
1958 Austin beat Fenwick
1959 Lane beat Fenwick

1960 Mt. Carmel beat Taft
1961 Weber beat Lane
1962 Fenwick beat Schurz
1963 St. Rita beat Vocational 42 to 7 in front of 81,270 on 11/30/63
1964 Weber beat Vocational
1965 Loyola beat Vocational
1966 Loyola beat Vocational
1967 Mt. Carmel beat Dunbar
1968 Mendel beat Vocational
1969 Loyola beat Lane

1970 St. Rita beat Lane 12 to 8
1971 St. Rita beat Morgan Park 18 to 12
1972 St. Laurence beat Taft
1973 St. Laurence beat Phillips
1974 St. Laurence beat Vocational
1975 Brother Rice beat Vocational
1976 Vocational beat St. Rita 13 to 6
1977 St. Rita beat Lane 20 to 8
1978 St. Laurence beat Sullivan
1979 Julian beat Joliet Catholic

1980 Brother Rice beat Julian
1981 Mt. Carmel beat Robeson
1982 Gordon Tech beat Julian
1983 Mt. Carmel beat Simeon
1984 De LaSalle beat Julian
1985 Mt. Carmel beat Lane
1986 Loyola beat Simeon
1987 Gordon Tech beat Julian
1988 Loyola beat Julian
1989 Julian beat Fenwick

1990 Robeson beat Gordon Tech
1991 Fenwick beat Bogan
1992 Mather beat Brother Rice
1993 Mt. Carmel beat Bogan
1994 Brother Rice beat Dunbar
1995 Loyola beat Julian
1996 Loyola beat Dunbar
1997 Dunbar beat Marian Catholic
1998 Hubbard beat Joliet Catholic
1999 Hubbard beat De La Salle

2000 Marion Catholic beat Simeon
2001 Mt. Carmel beat Morgan Park
2002 Carmel beat Dunbar
2003 Loyola beat Simeon
2004 Brother Rice beat Lane

With the 71st edition of the Chicago Prep Bowl in 2004, this match-up is one of the oldest in high school football. While football games between Catholic League teams and Public League teams pre-date the Chicago Prep Bowl, it wasn't until the leagues aligned their schedules and developed playoff formats that a City-wide championship could be held. The Public League has conducted 84 Public League City championships; the Catholic League, 81 City championships; this year was the 71st meeting of the two.

St. Rita has participated in five Chicago Prep Bowls, victorious on four occasions for a .833 winning percentage; in 71 years only two teams have won more Chicago Prep Bowls than St. Rita. St. Rita holds a number of spots in the all-time record books of the Chicago Prep Bowl, in a number of categories.

Most Points Scored in a Game –	St. Rita # 4 with 42 in 1963.
	Sister school Mendel is 5th with 41
Most Points Scored in a Game –	John Byrne of St. Rita # 1 with 36 in 1963
Most Touchdowns in a Game –	John Byrne of St. Rita # 1 with 5 (tie) in 1963
Most Yards Rushing in a Game –	John Byrne of St. Rita # 1 with 231 in 1963

Ever the team player, John Byrne ('64) would be the first to note that the undefeated season and National Championship in 1963 was a TEAM effort; running backs don't run unless offensive lines drive holes in the opposition, and offensive lines can't get the ball unless defensive lines take it away from the other guys. These modest statements would be made by all the St. Rita greats: the Dennis Licks, the Billy Mareks, the Mark Zavagnins and the John Foleys, to name just a few.

John R. Byrne ('64)   Dennis Lick ('72)   Bill Marek ('72)   Mark Zavagnin ('79)   John Foley ('86)

John Byrne ('64) (St. Margaret of Scotland) played college football at Indiana University; a knee injury ended his career, and he finished college at Loyola University in Chicago. Dennis Lick ('72) (St. Mary Star of the Sea) played his college ball at the University of Wisconsin, where he was a 1st Team All-American as a senior; upon graduation, he was a first round draft choice (8th) of the Chicago Bears, where he played for seven seasons. Bill Marek ('72) (Visitation) also played for and graduated from the University of Wisconsin; Bill was drafted as a free agent by the Bears. Mark Zavagnin ('79) (St. Bernadette) attended Notre Dame where, as a junior, he was an athletic and an academic All-American, and co-captain of the team; Mark was a 9th round draft choice of the Bears (11th) in 1983. John Foley ('86) played college ball at Notre Dame until a neck injury ended his playing days; John, who was the 1986 National High School player of the year at St. Rita, graduated from Notre Dame in 1990.

For decades, the Chicago Prep Bowl was considered the State championship, whether the winner was a Public League or Catholic League champion; attendance reports of the Illinois High School Association show the interest in this game.

Austin versus Leo in 1937 – attendance 110,000 est.
Leo versus Tilden in 1941 – attendance 95,000
Fenwick versus Schurz in 1962 – attendance 91,328
Fenger versus Weber in 1946 – attendance 85,000
Weber versus Lane in 1961 – attendance 83,750
St. Rita versus Vocational in 1963 – attendance 81,270
Fenger versus Mt. Carmel in 1938 – attendance 80,000
St. George versus Phillips in 1943 – attendance 80,000
Fenwick versus Tilden in 1945 – attendance 80,000

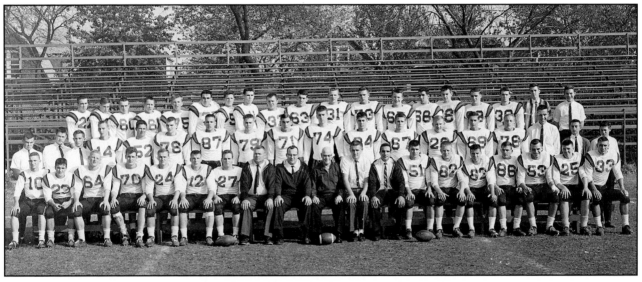

1963 Chicago Prep Bowl Champions - Defeated Chicago Vocational 42 to 7; selected National Champion High School Team by Associated Press. St. Rita's Prep Bowl victory came after taking the Chicago Catholic League crown from Loyola Academy by a score of 16 to 15, St. Rita's first CCL title in 40 years. The five staff members in the front row are, l to r, Head Coach Ed Buckley, Assistant Coach Bill Egan, Athletic Moderator Fr. Joseph O'Malley, Athletic Director Ed Galvin and Assistant Coach Jim Guzzo.

Playing in front of over 80,000 fans at Soldier Field had to be the thrill of a high school career. The picture at left shows part of the crowd at the 1963 Chicago Prep Bowl as a backdrop to St. Rita's #27 (John Byrne) squirting across the goal line on what turned out to be a busy day. Head Coach Ed Buckley called all the plays from the sidelines. The 1963 National Champion High School Team went 9 - 0 during the season, outscoring opponents 348 to 60.

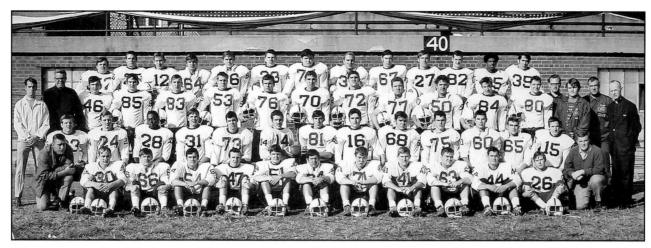

1970 Chicago Prep Bowl Champions - Defeated Lane Technical 12 to 8 in front of 65,735 after taking the Chicago Catholic League crown from Leo. St. Rita finished the season 9-2-1, avenging its losses to Leo and Loyola.

1971 Chicago Prep Bowl Champions - Defeated Morgan Park 18 to 12 in front of 43,175 after taking the Chicago Catholic League crown from Loyola. St. Rita finished the season at 12-0.

1977 Chicago Prep Bowl Champions - Defeated Lane Technical 20 to 8 in front of 23,400 beating the previously undefeated Public League Champs.

Everything changed in 1974 when the Illinois High School Association (I.H.S.A.) began a state series to insure state-wide representation. No longer would there be a single champion, but a number of champions according to school size; the State Series began with five classes in 1974, and has been expanded to eight classes by 2004; in the recent season, 549 teams competed in these eight classes, the top 256 advancing into the State Series. Through the 2004 series – the 31st Illinois State Tournament, St. Rita has made 20 appearances and holds a record of 34 wins and 18 losses.

St. Rita won the State Championship in 1978/79, and finished the season with a perfect 13 and 0 record. In that State Series St. Rita played in Class 5A and defeated Willowbrook, East St. Louis (Sr.), Richards and Buffalo Grove by a combined score of 113 to 21. St. Rita was the first Chicago school to capture the State title in football.

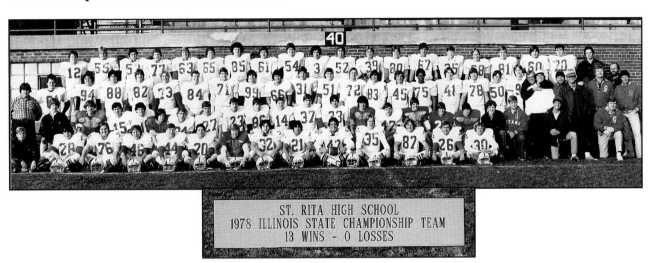

ST. RITA HIGH SCHOOL
1978 ILLINOIS STATE CHAMPIONSHIP TEAM
13 WINS - 0 LOSSES

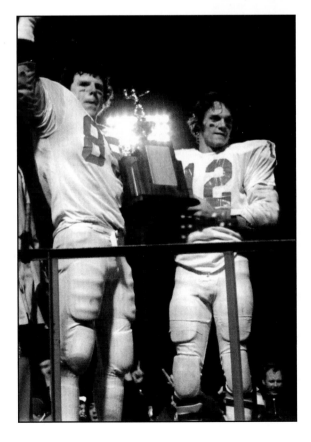

St. Rita Football - Head Coaches

Tom Shaughnessy	1920-1926
A.J. "Whitey" Cronin	1927-1929
Fr. Bill Donovan OSA	1930-1932
Dan Lamont	1933-1933
John "Hicks" Connelly	1934-1940
Dan Lamont	1940-1942
Leo Deutsch ('33)	1943-1946
Frank Mannott	1947-1948
Frank Kopczak	1949-1951
Robert Schultz	1952-1952
Ed Cody	1953-1955
Chuck Rheinschmidt	1956-1958
Ed Buckley	1959-1964
Jim Guzzo	1965-1966
Bill Styczynski	1967-1968
Pat Cronin (133 wins)	1969-1984
Todd Wernet ('75)(110 wins)	1985-1998
Todd Kuska ('90)	1999-

44-year old Head Coach Ed Buckley was a cigar-smoking, fedora-wearing former Marine Major who played his college ball at Harvard; he directed the 1963 National Championship team at St. Rita.

Head Coach Pat Cronin chalked up 133 wins in his 16 years at St. Rita; he was a four-time Tony Lawless Trophy winner as Outstanding Football Coach, and was elected to the CCL Hall of Fame.

Head Coach Todd Wernet ('75) guided teams for 13 years and won 100 games, with 10 state playoff appearances and six conference championships. Head Coaches Pat Cronin and Todd Wernet combined for 28 consecutive winning seasons.

CHICAGO SUN-TIMES

Chicago Sun-Times Player of the Year

1951 – Bob McKeiver, Evanston
1952 – Frank Pinn, Mt. Carmel
1953 – John Carroll, Fenwick
1954 – Jack Delveaux, Fenger
1955 – John Sawin, Vocational
1957 – Mike Lind, Calumet
1958 – Jack Strobel, Fenwick
1959 – Dick Butkus, Vocational
1960 – Al MacFarlane, Taft
1961 – Jim Grabowski, Taft
1962 – Jim DiLullo, Fenwick
1963 – John Byrne, St. Rita
1964 – Chico Kurzawski, Weber
1965 – LaMarr Thomas, Thornton
1966 – Randy Marks, Loyola
1967 – Tom Spotts, Maine South
1968 – Carlos Matthews, Evanston
1969 – Barry Cernoch, Downers Grove
1970 – Ken Ferguson, Lane Tech
1971 – Billy Marek, St. Rita
1972 – Jeff Stewart, Elk Grove
1973 – Kevin King, St. Laurence
1974 – Frank Shellenback, Barrington
1975 – Mark Carlson, Deerfield
1976 – Rich Weiss, New Trier
1977 – Chris Boskey, St. Francis de Sales
1978 – Marty Finan, Fenwick
1979 – Tim Marshall, Weber
1980 – Mike Tomczak, T.F. North
1981 – Tony Furjanic, Mt. Carmel
1982 – Eric Kumerow, Oak Park
1983 – Dempsey Norman, Tilden
1984 – Chuck McCree, Romeoville
1985 – John Foley, St. Rita
1986 – Kent Graham, Wheaton North
1987 – Jeff Lesniewicz, Homewood-Flossmoor
1988 – Brian Dunlavy, St. Viator
1889 – Alex Rodriguez, Lane Tech
1990 – Corey Rogers, Leo
1991 – Mike Alstott, Joliet Catholic
1992 – Broc Kreitz, Waubonsie Valley
1993 – Greg Williams, Bolingbrook
1994 – Jason Loerzel, Maine South
1995 – Tim Lavery, Naperville Central
1996 – Mark Floersch, New Trier
1997 – Rocky Harvey, Dunbar
1998 – Philip Macklin, Proviso East
1999 – Ryan Clifford, Naperville Central
2000 – Brett Basanez, St. Viator
2001 – Tim Brasic, Riverside-Brookfield
2002 – Tom Zbikowski, Buffalo Grove
2003 – Sean Price, Maine South
2004 – Chris Jeske, Joliet Catholic

GOLF

Golf is a sport in which St. Rita has a rich, but uneven history. St. Rita participated in the Chicago Catholic League golf conference, when Fr. Manny Gorra began the modern St. Rita golf program in 1962 (golf programs had been tried in the 1930/40's); disbanded in 1965, the golf team was resurrected between 1969 and 1975; it was restarted for the last time in 1978. St. Rita fields both junior varsity and varsity squads and is competitive every year. High school competition in golf dates back to the turn of the century, with the first state championship for individuals sponsored by the University of Illinois in 1916; state championships in a team format were added in 1938. The I.H.S.A. now sponsors the state tournament in two classes, A and AA; 522 high school teams competed in the most recent season.

1989/90 Sectional Qualifiers in Golf - 12 and 2 season record; Jim Prunty Head Coach.

Gymnastics

Gymnastics have had a following for a number of years. It is thought that the first interscholastic boy's gymnastics meet dates back to 1924, a Chicago Public League meet. The first statewide meet was in 1952, a University of Illinois sponsored invitational; six years later, the I.H.S.A. took over sponsorship of the state championships; 50 teams competed in the most recent season. While various events have come and gone over the years (for example, tumbling left in 1969 and trampoline was dropped in 1978), there now are six events to watch: floor exercise, pommel horse, still rings, vault, parallel bars and the horizontal bar. Competition is for individual events, and there also is an award for all-around performance.

Gymnastics has never been one of St. Rita's strengths, but that is not to say the school has not been to the mountaintop in this sport. While played on both a team and individual basis, there generally are not enough interested students at St. Rita to fill out an entire team; when the interest is there by an individual, St. Rita fully sponsors the effort.

In 1995/96, St. Rita came up with a superstar in the gymnastics arena in the form of Dave Johnson ('97). As a junior in 1995/96 Dave represented St. Rita in the individual events at the state championships. While finishing 1st in the floor exercise and still rings, Dave followed that up with 2nd place in the horizontal bar and the vault, and a 3rd in the parallel bars; all told, Dave Johnson earned 2nd all-around in the state championship in 1996, as St. Rita's lone entry. Dave still holds the state record (tie) in still rings, with a 9.80. Way to go Dave! A torn ACL crimped his performance in senior year.

Then and Now

After St. Rita, David Johnson ('97) went on to compete in gymnastics all four years he attended University of Illinois - Chicago; Dave was team captain in his senior year. Having graduated from UIC, Dave is returning to pursue a Masters degree. Pictured below is Dave on the still rings and, at right, accepting his championship medal at the I.H.S.A. state tournament in 1996.

Even earlier, St. Rita men would practice their sport with clubs and, after graduation, go on to star on the college level. One such case was Art Shurlock ('55); Art graduated St. Rita and attended the University of California on a gymnastics scholarship, where he won the NCAA pommel horse title in 1959; Art kept at his sport and represented the U.S. at the 1964 Olympics in Tokyo.

HOCKEY

Even though not an I.S.H.A.-sanctioned sport, ice hockey has long been a St. Rita strength. The Chicago Catholic Hockey League (CCHL) was formed for the 1963/1964 season, as was St. Rita hockey; the post-season CCHL Tournament was dubbed the Kennedy Cup (KC). St. Rita has played in ten KC finals, which are played in a best-of-three game format, winning three. The Amateur Hockey Association began sponsoring a State Championship in 1973/1974 in a single-elimination format; St. Rita played in three AAA Final Fours and two AA Final Fours, and won AAA State in 1981/1982; the Chicago Blackhawk Charities took over sponsorship in the 1996/1997 season.

KENNEDY CUP

1963/64	**Fenwick defeated St. Rita**
1964/65	Mt. Carmel
1965/66	Fenwick
1966/67	St. Laurence
1967/68	Fenwick
1968/69	Fenwick
1969/70	Brother Rice
1970/71	**Brother Rice defeated St. Rita**
1971/72	**Brother Rice defeated St. Rita**
1972/73	Mt. Carmel
1973/74	Mt. Carmel
1974/75	**St. Rita defeated Fenwick**
1975/76	Brother Rice
1976/77	Mt. Carmel
1977/78	Mt. Carmel
1978/79	Mt. Carmel
1979/80	Mt. Carmel
1980/81	Mt. Carmel
1981/82	Mt. Carmel
1982/83	**St. Laurence defeated St. Rita**
1983/84	**St. Rita defeated Mt. Carmel**
1984/85	Mt. Carmel
1985/86	Mt. Carmel
1986/87	**Mt. Carmel defeated St. Rita**
1987/88	Mt. Carmel
1988/89	Mt. Carmel
1989/90	Mt. Carmel
1990/91	Marist
1991/92	**St. Rita defeated Marist**
1992/93	Mt. Carmel
1993/94	Marist
1994/95	Marist
1995/96	Fenwick
1996/97	**Mt. Carmel defeated St. Rita**
1997/98	**Mt. Carmel defeated St. Rita**
1998/99	Mt. Carmel
1999/00	Mt. Carmel
2000/01	Brother Rice
2001/02	Loyola
2002/03	Fenwick
2003/04	Fenwick

STATE CHAMPIONSHIP

1973/74	Proviso West
1974/75	Oak Park/River Forest
1975/76	Notre Dame
1976/77	New Trier West
1977/78	Maine South
1978/79	Mt. Carmel
1979/80	Lyons Township
1980/81	New Trier East
1981/82	**St. Rita defeated Lyons Township**
1982/83	New Trier Green
1983/84	**Glenbrook North defeated St. Rita**
1984/85	Glenbrook North
1985/86	Mt. Carmel
1986/87	Mt. Carmel
1987/88	Mt. Carmel
1988/89	Glenbrook South
1989/90	Mt. Carmel
1990/91	Fremd
1991/92	Fremd
1992/93	Fremd
1993/94	New Trier Green
1994/95	Loyola-Gold
1995/96	Loyola-Gold
1996/97	Lake Forest Academy
1997/98	New Trier Green
1998/99	New Trier Green
1999/00	New Trier Green
2000/01	New Trier Green
2001/02	New Trier Green
2002/03	Fenwick
2003/04	Fenwick

Any discussion of St. Rita ice hockey has to include mention of Coach Jim Misiora ('67). Starting as a Varsity Assistant on the Kennedy Cup winning 1974/1975 team, Coach Mis was a part of practically every ice hockey trophy St. Rita ever brought home; he ended up elected to the CCHL Hall of Fame, on the strength of his 25 years of coaching and 500 wins (record – 500-376-84). Coach Mis graduated from St. Rita in 1967, completed his college work at Chicago State and began teaching at his alma mater in 1972, completing 30 years in education.

L to r, Jim Misiora as a St. Rita senior; as a varsity assistant, decked out in plaid with R. Schlender ('64) and J. Clifford 1975 Kennedy Cup coaches; and later in his career, offering some timely advice and counsel.

In over 40 years of hockey, St. Rita men have earned All-State selections many times.

Joe Patzin	1979/1980
Bob Valentine	1982
Dave Cronin	1982
Scott Paluch	1983
Brian Sabatino	1983
Jeff Bollman	1984
John Niestrom	1984
Jeff Schaaf	1984
Mike Wilford	1984
Rich Baran	1985
Dan Lopatka	1988
Chris Perillo	1988
Chris Galfano	1989
Jason Schlender	1989
Don Yurisich	1989
Mike Kelly	1990/1991
Chris Janoso	1993
Tony DaCosta	1993
Ryan Jestadt	1993
Aaron Gorecki	1994/1995
Brian Paolello	1994
Mike Schlie	1994/1995
Darcy Parsons	1995
Joe Caruso	1998
Bob McMillen	1998
Joe Weingart	2000

While length of season, competition quality and other factors weigh heavily on scoring, notching 50 goals in a high school season remains an accomplishment.

Jeff Schaaf	67 goals	83/84 Season
Joe Gotfryd	58 goals	74/75 Season
Joe Patzin	54 goals	78/79 Season
Rich Baran	51 goals	84/85 Season
Karl Pacini	50 goals	74/75 Season

Kennedy Cup Most Valuable Player

1975	Marty Kulikowski
1984	John Niestrom
1992	Mike Kelly

1974/75 Kennedy Cup Champions

1983/84 Kennedy Cup Champions

1991/92 Kennedy Cup Champions

St. Rita Ice Hockey Lifetime

Season	CCHL Record	Overall Record	Season	CCHL Record	Overall Record
1963/64	10-6-1 (4th)		1985/86	8-8-2 (xth)	18-17-3
1964/65	5-4-3 (5th)		1986/87	16-5-1 (2nd)	35-6-2
1965/66	4-10-3 (3rd)		1987/88	14-6-2 (3rd)	19-12-6
1966/67	6-5-1 (4th)		1988/89	11-10-1 (4th)	16-15-3
1967/68	DNP		1989/90	NA	
1968/69	6-5-0 (3rd)				
1969/70	5-6-1 (3rd)		1990/91	NA	
1970/71	7-10-0 (4th)		1991/92	11-5-7 (4th)	24-8-10
1971/72	6-9-1 (4th)		1992/93	12-8-2 (3rd)	25-15-4
1972/73	5-8-0 (4th)		1993/94	13-7-3 (3rd)	18-16-3
1973/74	6-7-1 (5th)		1994/95	(5th)	16-17-5
1974/75	17-4-1 (1st)	31-10-2	1995/96	7-9-4 (xth)	18-17-4
1975/76	10-8-0 (5th)	21-14-0	1996/97	13-12-2 (xth)	21-15-3
1976/77	4-15-1 (9th)	19-28-2	1997/98	NA	28-12-3
1977/78	12-9-3 (7th)	15-14-7	1998/99	(4th)	23-12-4
1978/79	3-16-1 (8th)	9-25-2	1999/00	⋆6-10-2 (6th)	14-18-3
1979/80	6-14-0 (7th)	14-24-1			
			2000/01	5-14-1 (6th)	16-19-4
1980/81	3-13-2 (7th)	10-20-2	2001/02	4-15-2 (7th)	13-25-3
1981/82	13-7-1 (3rd)	20-11-2	2002/03	6-13-1 (6th)	15-19-3
1982/83	18-5-2 (1st)	30-11-2	2003/04	4-13-2 (8th)	11-18-3
1983/84	24-1-0 (1st)	35-4-0	2004/05	8-12-0 (7th)	12-22-1
1984/85	12-9-5 (4th)	18-16-6			

CCHL Statistics include Kennedy CupGames.   ⋆ KennedyCup Game Missing

SOCCER

The I.H.S.A. has sponsored a state championship in boys soccer since the 1972/73 school year; interscholastic contests in soccer date back to 1909; in the most recent season, 375 teams competed at the state championships. St. Rita did not offer this brand of futbol in the early years of the school; St. Rita fielded its first team in soccer in 1968, founded by Br. Mark Thedens and Coach Nick Markulin. Since that first team, competition in the Chicago Catholic League conference has gotten better each year; St. Rita's 1976/77 team finished a good 2nd in the Catholic League; the 1977/78 team won St. Rita's first varsity soccer CCL championship. St. Rita made it as a Sweet 16 team in the 1982/83 season and won a regional berth in the state series during the 1990/91 season.

1977/78 Chicago Catholic League Champions - Head Coach Frank Aquilar

1982/83 I.H.S.A. Sweet 16 Soccer Team - Head Coach Br. Frank Paduch

1990/91 I.H.S.A. Regional Soccer Champions - Head Coach Stan Kastelic

SWIMMING

St. Rita swim teams were started by Fr. Richard Meehan in 1964, and continued through 1968. When St. Rita moved from its original location on 63rd and Oakley to the 77th and Western campus, the school gained a natatorium in the deal; after restarting with a club team, St. Rita re-entered competitive swimming in the Chicago Catholic League conference. As a school just returned to the sport, the swimmers know that experience and maturity will come with time; yet, the St. Rita teams have been competitive. On a statewide basis, the first interscholastic competition dates back to 1902, with the first state championships crowned during the 1931/32 school year; recently, 227 teams competed at state.

Shown above is the St. Rita natatorium on the 77th Street campus. One of the reasons swimming had trouble taking hold at 63rd Street was the lack of on-site facilities. With a pool on-site, swimming and water polo now flourish. At left is a picture of St. Rita's first state qualifier - Ed Gronkowski; Ed qualified for State in 2003/04 in the 50-yard freestyle by virtue of his win in the Orland Park Sectional with a time of 22.50; he finished a good 38th in State. At right is a view of a relay event.

TENNIS

Interscholastic competitive tennis in Illinois dates back more than a century; the first boy's tennis tournament for high schools is thought to be from 1894. The University of Illinois began sponsoring a statewide tennis tournament for individual competitors in 1911/12 school year; team competition began in 1935/36; at the most recent I.H.S.A. sponsored tournament, 283 schools competed for championships. At St. Rita, the school supports the sport when there are interested students, whether on a team or individual basis. Fr. John Patrick Murphy began the modern St. Rita tennis program in 1959/60 (previous tennis programs date to the 1940's), and interest remained through 1970. Athletic Director Mike Kisicki restarted both the golf and tennis programs in 1978. Tennis remained on the agenda until about 2000, when it was dropped due to lack of student interest. If interest does return, the school has a number of tennis courts at its 77th and Western campus, something it lacked at 63rd and Oakley.

The 1940/41 St. Rita tennis squad is pictured, believed to be the first team; tennis was started by Fr. J.P. Marron. L to r, Eckert, Hannon (Manager), Pukelis (Captain), Mancini and Imhof. At left is a picture showing the more modern version of a St. Rita tennis team.

TRACK & FIELD

Track and Field events date back more than a century, with the first Illinois meets in 1889; during the 1892/93 school year, the University of Illinois sponsored the first statewide track meet. Over the years many changes have taken place with events and format; for example, the bicycle used to be an event, but it was dropped in favor of discus in 1901; in 1914 the format was changed to two classes, returned to one class in 1926, and once again made two classes in 1975. Through it all, the level of competition has been striking; the 100th boy's state final was held in 1994; at the recent season, 569 high school teams competed in the I.H.S.A. sponsored state meet.

St. Rita has won a number of Chicago Catholic League meets and tournaments over the years, and been competitive in the high school arena. Since most Chicago-area Catholic teams didn't join the state competitions until the 1970's, St. Rita's claim of a 10.0 seconds mark in the 100-yard dash by John "Pie" Cranley in 1926 remains only a school record. St. Rita had a powerful presence in the 1920's in track, yet there was no Catholic league sponsorship as such, just a Catholic Meet until the modern era. Fr. John Burkhart started the modern era of St. Rita track & field in 1957, for both teams and individuals; since there aren't enough interested students to always fill out a full team, many times individuals are sponsored in individual events.

On an individual basis, St. Rita has had a number of Medalists at the state level, and two state championships by one individual – Tony Simmons, who earned four medals over two seasons. Tony still holds an individual top-ten record at state: tied for 5th all-time in the 100m dash with 10.2 seconds. Tony went on to star at track and football at the University of Wisconsin.

St. Rita Track & Field

Individual	Year	Event	Place
Relay Teams	1993	4x200 relay	6th
	1998	4x200 relay	7th
	1999	4x200 relay	6th
Sean Charles	1997	300m hurdles	4th
Dennis Crump	1997	100m dash	2nd
		200m dash	3rd
Tristan Geiger	1993	discus	2nd
Steve Kirwin	1983	300m hurdles	4th
Tom Knoebel	1980	shot put	5th
Ahmad Merritt	1994	long jump	7th
Kendall Perkins	1997	200m dash	8th
	1998	200m dash	6th
Tony Simmons	1992	100m dash	3rd
		200m dash	2nd
	1993	100m dash	1st
		200m dash	1st
Keith Thomas	1984	100m dash	2nd
Giles Travis	2000	long jump	8th

Tony Simmons ('93)

Tony Simmons was a multi-sport athlete at St. Rita in the early 90's. After graduation he attended the University of Wisconsin where he continued to shine; football ended up his sport. After a red-shirt freshman year, Tony starred the next four years as a Badger, finishing his career with 99 receptions for 1,991 yards and 23 TD's; the 23 TD's remains the record at Wisconsin. Tony was a 2nd round selection in the 1998 NFL draft; he played five years in the NFL with the Patriots, Colts and Giants; Tony also played in the NFL Europe with the Barcelona Dragons.

With strong individual performances in 1993 and 1997, St. Rita's Track & Field managed top-ten finishes at the state team championships: 4th place in state in 1993 and 7th place in 1997.

1993 Track Team - Finished 4th in I.H.S.A. State Finals under Head Coach Mike Murphy.

1953 Track Team

The brothers Eisenschenk - Sig ('65), on the left, and John ('72), on the right; both ran Cross Country and Track while at St. Rita. Sig (Team Captain as a senior) was mostly in distance events such as the City Relays (upper left hand corner of this page). John set three St. Rita records in one season: 50:09 in the 440, 2:00 in the 880, and 4:24.6 in the mile (lower left hand corner).

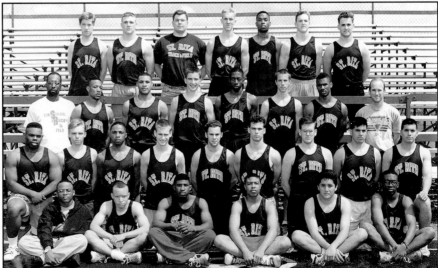

1994 Track Team - Chicago Catholic League Indoor and Outdoor Champions; Head Coach Mike Murphy.

VOLLEYBALL

Volleyball is one of those sports that have a recent, albeit rich, history. Volleyball teams have been around for years, yet a boys division did not gain state sponsorship until the 1991/92 school year; in the most recent season, 146 teams entered the state championships. If you've ever seen an interscholastic match in boy's volleyball, you know what real action is: slams, spikes, digs, kills, and aces; it is a game of speed and power.

St. Rita has sponsored a competitive volleyball team for years in the Chicago Catholic League and in state-wide play, and has been very successful; in four of the last five years, the St. Rita squad has earned berths in the state series; Coach Jim Palilonis and Coach Stan Kastelic each directed the St. Rita volleyball crew to the Elite-8 level at the state championships twice. The year 2001/02 proved to be the special one for the St. Rita volleyball men, as they placed 4th in State; the team won its quarterfinal game against Evanston Township, and then dropped the next set to eventual state champion Marist. With a return to the Elite-8 in the 2002/03 season, the St. Rita volleyball team set the I.H.S.A. record for consecutive Elite-8 appearances at four.

Under Head Coach Stan Kastelic, the 2002 Volleyball team set the St. Rita bar with a 4th Place finish in the State tournament. The team won both regional and sectional matches, and finished the year with a 28 - 14 record.

While the sport is young at St. Rita, it has been around long enough for the teams to have notched some individual and team top-ten places in the state records.

Most Aces in a Match – 4th highest at 9 – Ryan Biros against Evanston on May 31, 2002
Most Kills in a Season – 8th highest at 1,407 – 2002/03 season
Fewest Points Allowed, Match – tied for 1st at 0 – against St. Gregory on March 22, 2000
Most Elite-8 Appearances – 4th at 4 – 1999/00, 2001, 2002 and 2003
Consecutive Appearances – 1st at 4 – 1999/00, 2001, 2002 and 2003

Stan Kastelic ('78) is one of those dedicated Ritamen *who came back to his alma mater after college; besides more than 15 years of teaching, Coach Kastelic has moderated or coached a number of activities: Billiards, Canoe & Hiking, Soccer, Golf, Tennis, Racquetball, and found some of his greatest success in Volleyball. As Head Coach of Volleyball, his teams earned two of St. Rita's four consecutive Elite-8 appearances in State competition, one of which ended up with a berth in the final four.*

2000 Volleyball with Head Coach Jim Palilonis; Regional and Sectional Champions - Elite 8 appearance.

2001 Volleyball; Regional and Sectional Champions - Elite 8 appearance.

Jim Palilonis' first season coaching with St. Rita was the 1998/99 Volleyball squad. After his first year, Coach Palilonis led the Team to its first two Elite-8 appearances (1999/00 and 2000/01). Above is a picture of the Coach leading practice. Coach Palilonis ended up with a 66-37 record in volleyball at St. Rita.

2003 Volleyball; Regional and Sectional Champions - Elite 8 appearance.

Water Polo

With access to its own natatorium after the move from 63rd Street, St. Rita began a club team in water polo; this team rose to competitive status in 1991 when the school began competition in the Chicago Catholic League. While water polo has been played at the Chicago Catholic League conference level for years, it was not a sponsored sport at the state level because of the relatively few schools that offered competitive level of play; in these early days, whichever team won the Illinois Swimming Association title was the de facto state champion; this changed during the 2001/02 school year when a state championship tournament was organized under the aegis of the I.H.S.A.; in the most recent season, 56 teams vied for the state championship. While it did not take home the laurels, St. Rita competed in that first state series and has ever since. As experience is gained, look for St. Rita swimmers and water polo competitors to achieve more success. In 1999, Michael Cashman ('99) was a first team selection on the All-American Boys Water Polo Team by the National Interscholastic Swimming Coaches Association.

St. Rita Water Polo History

Year	Record
1990/91	7-13
1991/92	14-8
1992/93	9-16
1993/94	9-15
1994/95	12-19
1995/96	17-11
1996/97	8-13
1997/98	10-13
1998/99	17-6-2
1999/00	21-9
2000/01	13-13
2001/02	14-13-1
2002/03	11-16
2003/04	10-15

1992 Illinois Swimming Association Southern Division Champions

Pictured above is Coach Chuck Knibbs, the only coach Water Polo has ever had. At left, Mike Cashman ('99) who, with or without a tie, was a player. Besides being named All-Conference, All-State and All-American in his senior year, Mike found time to be Class President and earn a Scholastic Award...now that's an All-Around performance.

WRESTLING

Wrestling has been a high school sport for many years; it is believed that competition between high schools dates back to 1926. Oftentimes, football athletes take up wrestling so they can work on their strength and conditioning; it is a complementary sport. St. Rita introduced its program beginning in the 1984/85 school year. John Pfeffer ('88) and Br. John Newton get credit for starting the wrestling program and for keeping it breathing during some hard times early on; the current coach Dan Carroll gets credit for bringing St. Rita's program up to another level of play.

In the early years of competitive wrestling, the sport was conducted on an individual basis with medalists crowned in separate weight divisions; as interest in the sport grew, the number of weight divisions increased to the current 14 classes. The first state-sponsored wrestling meet for individuals dates back to 1937; in 1974, the sport was split into two classes, A and AA; St. Rita competes in Class AA. In 1984, a team format was added to wrestling, called dual-meet, where a line-up of wrestlers in the various weight divisions would meet another school's line-up; in the most recent season, 392 schools fielded teams in the state tournament.

As an individual sport, St. Rita has had twenty three medalists over the years; included among these were three state champions.

Student	Season	Weight Class	State Finish
Mike Boyd	1999	145	2nd
	2001	145	1st
Fred Deramus	2003	275	4th
	2004	275	3rd
Bob Fangerow	2003	135	3rd
Adam Gonzalez	2001	152	3rd
Mike Justich	2003	130	4th
Dan Keenan	2003	171	5th
Ryan Klinger	2001	119	4th
	2002	119	1st
	2003	125	5th
Dan Manzella	2001	103	5th
	2002	112	2nd
	2003	119	3rd
John Murphy	2002	160	6th
	2003	160	6th
	2004	171	2nd
Jay O'Malley	2001	135	5th
Scott Sands	2004	189	3rd
Obie Simpson	2004	152	6th
John Starzyk	2004	103	4th
Matt Vaci	2003	140	2nd
Albert White	2004	135	1st

Mike Boyd ('01) (Our Lady of the Snows Parish) was St. Rita's first individual state champion; as a senior in 2000/01 Mike finished first while competing at 145 lbs. Mike now attends the University of Illinois - Champaign where he wrestles at 157 pounds.

Ryan Klinger ('03) (St. Linus Parish) earned 1st Place at 119 pounds as a junior in 2002; Ryan was St. Rita's second individual medalist. Ryan is on the wrestling team at the University of Illinois - Champaign where he wrestles at 133 pounds.

Albert White (Class of 2007) is St. Rita's third individual state champion; competing as a freshman, Albert went a perfect 50 and 0 in 2003/04 and placed 1st in 135 pound class.

On a dual-meet basis, St. Rita has advanced to regional champion three times, 2001, 2003 and 2004. In 2001, the team won regional and sectional championships, advancing it to the quarterfinals at State, where they lost a close match to Glenbard North. The experience was incalculable.

2000/01 Regional and Sectional Champions AA Dual Meet Wrestling

In 2003, St. Rita was not to be denied. Winning regional and sectional titles to earn their way into the quarterfinals at State, St. Rita went on to take quarters, semis and the championship. Beating sister school Providence added measurably to the victory. Under Coach Dan Carroll, St. Rita defeated an unbeaten DeKalb in the quarterfinals, a strong team from Conant in the semi-finals, and Providence Catholic in the finals, in a series that wasn't decided until the last two matches. It truly was a team performance, as St. Rita became state champion without having a single individual state champion ...**St. Rita 2003 State Champion** in dual meet wrestling.

2002/03 I.H.S.A. AA Dual Meet State Wrestling Champion

In 2004, St. Rita decided they liked what they experienced the previous year and they wanted more. Having tasted victory, the Team added a lot of drama to its quest for a second consecutive dual meet State championship. While the Team had one individual state champion (Albert White at 135 lbs.), its performance in the dual meet at state was exceptional. Given the 14 weight classes (103, 112, 119, 125, 130, 135, 140, 145, 152, 160, 171, 189, 215 and 275 lbs.), the dual meet was wrestled across those same weights. After dispatching Notre Dame and Glenbard North in the quarterfinals and semi-finals, St. Rita began its pursuit of a second state title in the finals by losing six of the first seven matches, falling behind 22 to 4; only a perfect finish in the last seven matches would give them a chance…and that is just what they made happen, winning six of the next six to draw into its first lead, albeit a slim one at 24 to 22; with all the pressure on the last match for the dual meet title, St. Rita completed its seven for seven finish, once again beating sister school Providence, this time by 27 to 22. Out of 14 matches, only four were major decisions, and St. Rita nabbed three of those. **St. Rita 2004 State Champion** in dual meet wrestling.

The Road to Moline

Sectionals		State Final Tournament			State Champion
Hoffman Estates (Conant)	Libertyville 31-31	Fox Lake (Grant) 33-26	Carpentersville (Dundee-Crown) 33-28	New Lenox (Providence Catholic) 35-30	
Libertyville					
Fox Lake (Grant)	Fox Lake (Grant) 30-29				
Wheeling					
Belvidere	Sterling (H.S.) 42-27	Carpentersville (Dundee-Crown) 35-30			
Sterling (H.S.)					
Crystal Lake (South)	Carpentersville (Dundee-Crown) 48-24				
Carpentersville (Dundee-Crown)					New Lenox (Providence Catholic) 35-30
Orland Park (Sandburg)	New Lenox (Providence Catholic) 30-19	New Lenox (Providence Catholic) 55-8	New Lenox (Providence Catholic) 38-21		
New Lenox (Providence Catholic)					
South Holland (Thornwood)	Frankfort (Lincoln-Way East) 46-30				
Frankfort (Lincoln-Way East)					
Mahomet (M.-Seymour)	Minooka 34-30	Minooka 31-26			
Minooka					
East Peoria	Bloomington (H.S.) 32-31				Chicago (St. Rita) 27-22
Bloomington (H.S.)					
Niles (Notre Dame)	Niles (Notre Dame) 40-33	Niles (Notre Dame) 30-28	Chicago (St. Rita) 57-11	Chicago (St. Rita) 37-18	
Evanston (Twp.)					
Oak Park (O.P.-River Forest)	Bensenville (Fenton) 27-25				
Bensenville (Fenton)					
Chicago (Gordon Tech)	Chicago (St. Rita) 56-12	Chicago (St. Rita) 48-18			
Chicago (St. Rita)					
Berwyn-Cicero (Morton)	Chicago (Mt. Carmel) 39-26				
Chicago (Mt. Carmel)					
LaGrange (Lyons)	Maywood (Proviso East) 39-30	Carol Stream (Glenbard North) 30-28	Carol Stream (Glenbard North) 31-30		
Maywood (Proviso East)					
Carol Stream (Glenbard North)	Carol Stream (Glenbard North) 34-33				
Naperville (Neuqua Valley)					
Belleville (Althoff)	Granite City 44-19	Granite City 64-5			
Granite City					
Jacksonville (H.S.)	Jacksonville (H.S.) 49-18				
Murphysboro					

OTHER SPORTS

The St. Rita athletic program has always matched the activities offered to the interests of the student body. As teenager's wants and desires changed over the years, different sports have been added or dropped to keep up with the times. Boxing and Rifle were two sports that had a memorable past at St. Rita but were not of interest these days, and were dropped from interscholastic competition. Boys volleyball was just the opposite, being started in 1992 with state sponsorship because of the growing interest at many schools.

BOXING

In times past, boxing was a big sport for youth; one reason for this interest was the low cost for equipment, usually just gloves. Many high schools had intramural programs and, as more and more schools took part, tournaments were started. The Catholic Youth Organization (C.Y.O.) tournament for the Archdiocese often drew 200 to 300 boxers. St. Rita used Harris Gym as the site for its boxing matches; St. Rita conducted intramural boxing for years, the best of those then joined the competitive boxing team for interscholastic contests. The *Golden Gloves* amateur boxing competition in Chicago was started in 1923 at the Chicago Stadium; *Golden Gloves* south sectional competitions spent most of the 1940's and 1950's at St. Rita's Harris' Gym, as did some C.Y.O. meets. For example, in the 1956 *Golden Gloves* 245 boxers sought titles; these boxers came from high schools (such as the 14 from St. Rita), private boys clubs (such as Valentine Boys Club), various C.Y.O. and Y.M.C.A. clubs, and surrounding states (such as the Twin City Boys Club from East Chicago, Indiana). The south-side *Golden Gloves* sectional at St. Rita had 114 boys registered, while the north-side tournament at St. Andrews gym had 131 boxers; contested over three days, each site would send 16 fighters (8 open and 8 novice division) to St. Andrews gym for the City finals; the eight City finals open division champions would represent Chicago in the 32-city Tournament of Champions (started in 1928), sponsored by the *Chicago Tribune Charities*, at the Chicago Stadium. Boxing was BIG.

St. Rita had dropped boxing from its athletic schedule during the war years (1943/44 and 1944/45); all that changed when a new priest was appointed to the St. Rita faculty in June, 1945 - 28-year old Father Francis P. Crawford. Once settled in at St. Rita High School, the former amateur middleweight boxer from Pennsylvania restarted his favorite sport. Over the next ten years, Father Crawford's boxing program at St. Rita would generate a stream of C.Y.O and Golden Gloves champions.

St. Rita Boxing – City Champions
Mel Gordon 1947 *Golden Gloves* @118 lbs
Don Schuster 1948 *Golden Gloves* @ lightheavy
Ed Curley 1950 *Golden Gloves* @118 lbs
John Werbach 1951 *Golden Gloves* @147 lbs
Bob Jemilo 1952 *Golden Gloves* @112 lbs
Chuck Blasco 1955 *Golden Gloves* @118 lbs
Louis Beuschlein 1956 *Golden Gloves* @112 lbs

Dick Jemilo 1948 C.Y.O. @135 lbs
Jake Solus 1948 C.Y.O. @ lightheavy
Ed O'Callaghan 1951 C.Y.O. @135 lbs
Frank Walsh 1951 C.Y.O. @175 lbs
Bob Jemilo 1952 C.Y.O. @112 lbs
Ken Kaner 1953 C.Y.O. @ lightweight
George Jurinek 1954 C.Y.O. @112 lbs
Ken Kaner 1954 C.Y.O. @147 lbs
Jack Cavanaugh 1955 C.Y.O. @112 lbs
Al Srupsa 1955 C.Y.O. @118 lbs

Boxing was practiced through individual schools and clubs, and through a few major outlets: the C.Y.O. competitions, the *Golden Gloves* tournaments and the St. Rita Invitational. Shortly after St. Rita restarted its boxing program, it initiated the St. Rita Invitational in the Winter of 1946, and then won it for the next seven straight years (through the 1952/53 school year); with the St. Rita Invitational came the *Gardner Trophy,* which was donated by Dr. James Gardner ('29) and his brother Andrew "Bud" Gardner ('26); the trophy was awarded to the school winning the team competition.

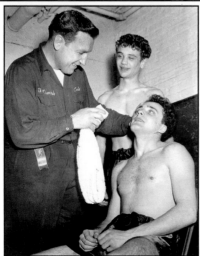

Like any good coach, Father Francis P. Crawford was there for his student/ athletes. Whether he was working the fighter's corner as his Second (above) or cleaning him up between bouts (left), Father Crawford's boxers always knew he was in there with them. Picture left, Chicago Tribune *Photo.*

Year after year St. Rita would field boxing teams at major tournaments, such as C.Y.O. and *Golden Gloves*. Oftentimes, the school earned an award for fielding the largest number of boxers; it was not unusual for St. Rita to have a good fighter registered for each and every division, both novice and open; this meant St. Rita would bring squads of 16 or more boxers to each meet.

Today some of that rich tradition can still be found at St. Rita's gym. While boxing is no longer sponsored as an interscholastic sport, clubs and private gyms have taken over that role.

Then and Now

Louis Beuschlein, who won the 112 lbs. Golden Gloves City Championship in the Open Division in 1956, would be the first to tell you he couldn't make the weight today; but in 1956, he had the 'right stuff'. Shown above, l to r, Louis as a senior at St. Rita; in fighting form posed working the heavy bag; slipping one punch while landing his own; and as he looks today. Having taken enough blows to the head, Louis turned down a boxing scholarship from the University of Wisconsin and went to Beloit College, from which he graduated in 1960. During his 30 year teaching career in the south suburbs, he picked up a Master's degree too.

RIFLE

One sport that would be considered politically incorrect to teach youth today is that of shooting sports, particularly rifle competition; but handled and taught with respect, rifle competition indeed is a worldwide sport, even an Olympic sport. Rifle competition was offered at St. Rita between 1964 and 1968, moderated by Fr. Joseph O'Malley and Br. Joseph Fisher. The group competed against clubs such as Downer's Grove, Morton Grove, Villa Park, DePaul ROTC, Lawndale Boys Club, Southtown YMCA and the University of Chicago club. St. Rita was serious about rifle and Fr. O'Malley eventually became a state certified rifle instructor; St. Rita held the 1965 NRA Junior Sectionals. The rifle club worked with the Southtown Y.M.C.A., from which it could borrow rifle equipment and access a shooting range.

The 1965 Red Team: Front, l to r, J. Prazuck, R. Kmiec, P. Graham; Back, R. Lamb, J. Maksym, Bro. Joseph, J. Moone and S. Olejnik.

The 1965 Blue Team: R. Wojcik, J. Kochan, W. Brady, J. Chepon; Back, A. Copack, R. Kosinski, S. Bylina, R. Plaza and T. Winski.

The St. Rita Rifle Club also performed at football games as the Rifle Drill Team in conjunction with the Color Guard. Shown at attention above, note there was one left-handed member, at second from right.

ACTIVITIES AT ST. RITA

In extra-curricular activities, St. Rita sponsors many athletic programs and a number of specialized activities, some state sponsored and others not. Similar to sports, these activities play a big part in the development of the whole student; it is not so important which extra-curricular activity a student chooses to round out his education, just that he chooses some.

St. Rita sponsors of number of state-recognized activities: cheerleading, chess, music, and scholastic bowl; chess and scholastic bowl are sponsored by the I.H.S.A. with statewide competitions leading up to state championships. St. Rita also has had a band program for decades; whether accompanying the sports activities or firmly established in its own right, band continues to shine.

BAND

St. Rita has been blessed with a strong Band program for more than 50 years. Bob Black ('40) came back to his *alma mater* in 1946 to help start the modern marching band program; after some years, Louis Ricci ('53) took over direction for more than 25 years. Today's band curriculum is led by Cindy Gradek, with the assistance of Jodi McLawhorn, both graduates of DePaul University's VanderCook School of Music. While names change - Marching, Concert, Swing, Stage, All-Star, Dance, Music, Jazz and Symphony bands – today there is a full spectrum of music at St. Rita; major trips are taken every other year to showcase the band…in 2005 the Band will sojourn to Cascia, Italy, the home of our Patroness.

Over the years, St. Rita's Band has performed as the Honor Band for President Kennedy (10/1963), the half-time show at the NFL Championship Game in Green Bay (1/1966) and the Home Band (Marching Mascots) for the Chicago Cardinals NFL football team – besides appearing at McCormick Place, Riverview, Holy Cross Hospital, DisneyWorld, City Hall and numerous other venues.

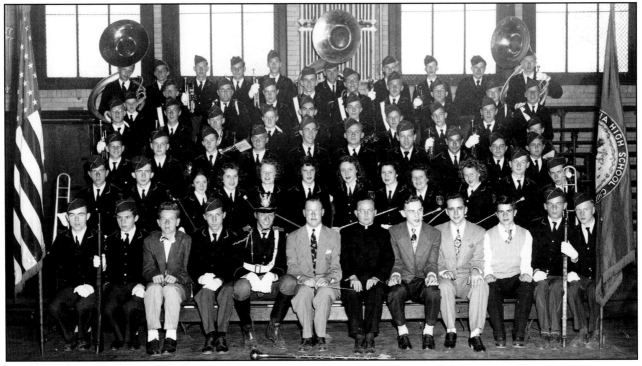

One of the earliest of the St. Rita Marching Bands - this one in the 1947/48 school year. Mr. Bob Black ('40), Band Director, sits front and center.

The first St. Rita Band was formed during the 1929/30 school year through the efforts of Father Peter Paul. The picture above shows the Band the next school year (1930/31); Mr. H. Bachman was named Director and Instructor, Fr. Paul remained as Moderator. The two pictures below show the 2003/04 school year version - the Marching Band on top and the Symphony on bottom.

Ray Manzarek '56 (center) finally got to play in the St. Rita Band; Assistant Director Jodi McLawhorn (far left) and Director Cindy Gradek (lower right).

1977/78 School Year - St. Rita High School Band and Ritanettes

Early 1950's Marching Band; front and center is Director Bob Black and, on his right, is future Band Director Louis Ricci ('53).

1958/59 School Year

Red Pastorek ('58) was a product of St. Turibius Parish and attended St. Rita in the middle fifties; he played bass in the dance band at the end of Bob Black's tenure and, in Red's senior year, played for Louis Ricci who had taken over band direction. After high school, Red attended De Paul University, then went on the road with various dance bands, had a stint at the Florida Symphony and, in 1964, began a career with the Houston Symphony Orchestra; Red celebrated his 40th Anniversary with the Houston Symphony Orchestra, where he plays double bass.

RITANETTES

John Reilly Photograph

Whether accompanying the Marching Band or performing on their own, the Ritanettes *take a back seat to no one.* Ritanettes, *in one form or another, have been a part of St. Rita almost as long as the band program. When Bob Black stepped down from Band Director, he took up leading the* Ritanettes. *Shown above are early versions, circa 1950's on the left and 1960's on the right and, below, a more modern team. Composed of young women from the surrounding high schools, the* Ritanettes *were not without their famous alumnae; Anne McGlone (Maria High School) was a* Ritanette *in the 1960's; she is shown above, next to last in the lineup on the right; as a sophomore in 1959/60, she was St. Rita's Homecoming Queen. Off to DePaul and then Kent College of Law, she married Alderman Edward Burke, was appointed to the Bench in 1987 and has sat on the Appellate Court since 1995 - not a bad start for a* Ritanette. *She is shown in a current picture at far left.*

CHEERLEADING

While it is only recently that the I.H.S.A. began to sponsor Cheerleading as an activity, that is not to say that there was little interest. Cheerleading, which originally was to lead and direct the cheering at high school athletic events, has grown over the years. From simple cheers, to coordinated steps and cheers, to today's tumbling and complex choreographed routines, cheerleading has grown nationwide; state and national cheerleading competitions are held throughout the country during the year. St. Rita is fortunate to always have had young women from the surrounding high schools interested enough to form teams and represent the *Mustangs*. In 2001/02, the St. Rita cheerleaders won a regional competition of the National Cheerleaders Association (NCA) at Purdue University, gaining them a bid for the NCA Nationals; at Nationals in Dallas the *Cheering Mustangs*, composed of 22 young women from five different high schools (Mother McAuley, Queen of Peace, Maria, Mt. Assisi and Trinity), took the gold. From yesterday to today, cheerleading continues to be a big part of St. Rita sports.

...and lest anyone think that all Cheer Leaders wore skirts, this picture shows the 1940/41 version: l to r, O'Connor, Davin, Lebert and Curtis.

St. Rita Cheerleaders - 2001/02 NCA National Champions. L to r, seated: Nicole Denton, Celina Saenz, Vanessa Villa, Liz Dabrowski, Allison Venegas, Andrea Venegas, Katie Coyle and Krista Placas; kneeling: Allison Donenberg, Nicole Rafalin, Mary Murphy, Meaghan Guilfoyle, Stephanie Sterk and Michelle Dudek; standing: Michelle Fieldman, Laura Koszulinski, Chelsea Fahey, Rachel Koszulinski, Jacyln Schuld and Erica Richey.

CHESS

Chess is an I.H.S.A. sponsored activity that competes statewide; the first state championships were held in 1975; in the most recent season, 118 teams from across Illinois vied for the state trophy; St. Rita finished 56th in the 2002/03 state competition. St. Rita first entered competition in the Chicago High School Chess Conference in 1966/67; in that first year St. Rita finished in first place in the South Section beating Brother Rice, Hales and Mendel each twice, while splitting with St. Laurence.

1966/67 practice session, presided over by Moderator Ron Dvorak.

John Klein ('98) was a super-soph when it came to Chess. In 1995/96, competing as an individual, John won the Illinois State Chess Championship at the tournament held at Illinois State University. The team won the CCL South Section title.

1980/81 Chicago Catholic League South Section Champions

1981/82 Chicago Catholic League Champions; this Team finished 12th out of 75 teams in State competition. From l to r, at bottom Mike McGriff, Bob Spontak, Karolis Drunga; at top, Dan Vohasek, Gerard Jungeman, Jurgis Drunga, Bill Grady and Moderator/Coach Norb Lasky.

1993/94 Chicago Catholic League Champions

SCHOLASTIC BOWL

Scholastic Bowl is a state-sponsored activity that St. Rita has participated in for many years. The first state championships were held in 1987; St. Rita has taken honors in conference play in the 1990/91 season and, in the 1998/99 season, it took Regional Honors at the State level. Besides state competition, St. Rita competes in the Southwest Metropolitan Scholastic Bowl Conference, an organization of 12 schools from the greater Chicago-area Catholic Leagues. In the most recent season, 208 schools competed for the state trophy.

The St. Rita Scholastic Bowl teams work hard at improving their results. At upper right is Ms. Lubke with a practice set-up during the season. At lower right, Mrs. Sally Deenihan, who moderated the team in the early years, poses with the 1989/90 Scholastic Bowl squad.

The St. Rita muses took Regional Honors in the I.H.S.A. State series in 1998/99. Shown with Coach Lynn Lubke are, l to r, seated - Joe Caesar, Tim Garcia and Alan Michalski; standing - Jonathan Grill, Randy Hall, Devin Hester and James Leiser. St. Rita defeated Reavis, Oak Lawn and St. Laurence to take the regional title.

The 2004/05 version of the Scholastic Bowl team is moderated by Mr. Joe Partacz, front and center in the picture above. The team is shown at the Richards Invitational in 2004, an invitational tournament of 64 schools.

HEENEY AWARDS

The Heeney Award recognizes achievement in academics at St. Rita. When the Award originated in 1968 it was given to the top student in each class, to four *Ritamen* each semester; later, it was changed to an honor bestowed on each student who maintained straight A's for the semester. The Award is named in honor of a past President of the Fathers' Club, Mr. Joseph Heeney.

The photograph at left shows the first Heeney Awards *being presented. The picture dates to early-1968, when Mrs. Helen Heeney conferred the awards on the St. Rita students who finished ranked first in their respective classes. L to r, senior Audrius Plioplys, junior Gary Sladek, sophomore Adrian Soprych and freshmen (tied) Thomas Baltutis and Martin Baunbach; Father William Thomas, Ed Poetz and John Hohol look on at right.*

Shown below is a current view of the Heeney Award *ceremony. Joe and Helen Heeneys' son Michael Heeney ('71) carries on the tradition of presenting the Award, and the Fathers' Club carries on the tradition of sponsoring the event, now in its 38th year.*

...there are no cheering crowds, no pep rallies and no golden trophies to urge you on. You have to find the great desire for excellence within yourself...mk

DRAMA CLUB

Putting on formal Plays with Casts and Stage Hands and Sets had been an on-and-off occurrence at St. Rita during the early years; organization and direction being the hold back. With the arrival of Fr. Seary a formal Dramatic Club was organized during the 1927/28 and, with some regularity since then, an annual play has been a mainstay of the School – sometimes two a year. Today it is called the Drama Club, led by Connie Johnston for the last eight years. There also are outlets for student improv and stand-up comedy.

Cast and Crew of "Monday, Always Leads to Murder".

CAST OF "AARON BOGGS, FRESHMAN"

Aaron Boggs.................................James Sullivan
Jimmie Jamieson...................Thomas McWilliams
Beau Carter....................................Peter Kuhl
Pepper Jarvis...........................Martin McCarthy
Epenetus P. Boggs.................Thomas P. Ouska
Mr. Chubb.........................Bartholomew Ahern
Casey Jones............................Joseph LeBlanc
Second Hand Abey........................Thomas Nash
Elyzabethe Feeny......................William Halpin
Mrs. Chubb..............................Thomas Hynes
Mrs. Pickens..........................Thomas Powers
Miss Evelyn Newcomb..................Joseph Fenlon
Lois Hunter................................George McMahon
Cherry Carruthers......................Donald Wickers
Loretta Rea..................................James Gibson
Miss Dollie de Cliffe....................Joseph Glynn

GLEE CLUB

John Muellman, Theodore Lownik, Herbert Stalzer, Francis Foran, William Moran, Joseph Kean, John Donovan, Myles Gibbons, Andrew Friedrich

STAGE ASSISTANTS

John Niedbala, Frank Foster, George Krieps, Mason Cronin, Edward Dolinski

1930/31 Dramatic Club production under Father Seary.

The St. Rita of Cascia
High School
Drama Club
Proudly Presents

YOU CAN'T TAKE IT WITH YOU

by George S. Kaufman and Moss Hart

April 7, 2000 7:30pm
April 8, 2000 7:30pm
April 9, 2000 2:00pm

St. Rita Auditorium
7740 S. Western Avenue, Chicago

Connie Johnston

1999/2000 Drama Club production under Mrs. Connie Johnston

OTHER CLUBS & ACTIVITIES

In the greater scheme of things, many Clubs and Organizations came and went over the years at St. Rita. Activities were always tailored to the interests of the boys, and those changed over time; some of the clubs were started, stopped and restarted at later times. But there always were a number of activities in which one could get involved. Clubs such as: Aviation Club, Billiards Club, Biology Club, the *Cascian*, Chess Club, Comic Book Club, Debating Club, Dramatic Club, Flying & Gliding Club, French Club, Glee Club, Guitar Club, History Club, the literary journal *Inscape*, Monogram Club, Photography Club, Radio Club, Rita A-Go-Go Club, the *Ritan*, Science Club, Ski and Camping Club, Stamp and Coin Club, Stock Club, Street Hockey Club, Chorus and the Student Broadcasting System (SBS). And then there are the activities that have social significance, such as S.A.D.D. and the Knights of Augustine.

Two 1930's clubs: St. Rita Debating Club, on the left, and Glee Club with Father Seary, on the right

The Knights of Augustine (K of A) was a fraternal organization at St. Rita; over the years the K of A has had a big following in some periods and faded out in others; today it is being revived on the campus under the direction of Brother Jerome Sysko. The picture above is from the K of A group during the 1980/81 school year when the brotherhood had 72 students enrolled and six faculty advisors; in the center of the picture was a guest speaker, the Very Reverend Arthur Ennis, Assistant General of the English Speaking Provinces of the Order of St. Augustine; to his immediate left was a future St. Rita principal - sophomore Tom McCarthy; and, at third from right in the top row, was a future St. Rita assistant principal - senior Wes Benak. The purpose of the K of A was to help the students grow together in brotherhood, sharing their time and talents to help others, such as in toy drives and canned food drives; they also helped with religious services and special school activities. The K of A members acted as secular Augustinians.

The St. Rita Stock Club, moderated by Mr. Rich Grill ('64) since its inception in 1974; originally the Club bought and sold actual stocks through Merrill, Lynch; today it is a computer simulation sponsored by the Illinois Council on Economic Education. In 2002/03 the St. Rita Stock Club placed 1st out of 130 teams in the Chicago High School Division and 44th out of 1,691 in Illinois; l to r, the winning students are Pat Malone, Sean Murphy, Jonathon Butkus and Jerome Howard.

These five pictures, clockwise from upper left: Illinois State Scholars group, moderated by Joe Bamberger; the Canoe and Hiking Club, moderated by Stan Kastelic; the Billiards Club, also moderated by Stan Kastelic; S.A.D.D. making a point with their "Dead-for-a-Day" program and moderated by Mike Kisicki; and the Astronomy club, moderated by Rachel Jarosik.

School Dances

Whether its called a Senior Prom, a Junior Prom, Mother/Son Dance, Frosh/Soph Date Dance, Christmas Ball, Student Council Dance, Spring Band Festival, Mixer, Sock Hop or even Computer Dance – there were a number of ways for young men to get together with their young women. Whether in the Grand Ballroom of the Morrison Hotel or the school gym, school dances were a mainstay of high school life.

HOMECOMING

Homecoming always has had a special meaning. Unless one saw it first hand, one really couldn't appreciate the pomp and circumstance. Over the years it has included bonfires in the stadium, concerts with acts such as The Guess Who, REO Speedwagon and the like, and special appearances by notables such as Larry Lujack and Steve Dahl. The Mustang Stampede said it all.

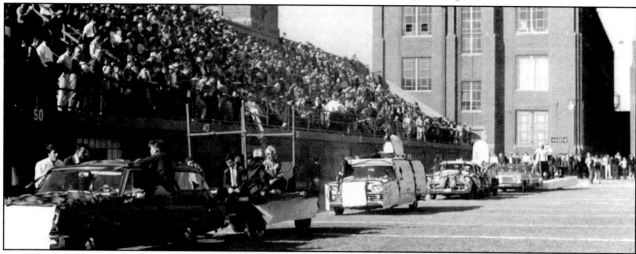

14TH WARD FOOTBALL DAY

John Kelly Photograph

Affiliations come and go over the years, and St. Rita has been blessed with many. One such relationship has been with the 14th Ward Regular Democratic Organization, which began scheduling a Football Day each year to celebrate their activities and success with the people who made it possible. While the Football Day originally moved from venue to venue, with the arrival of freshman Alderman Edward M. Burke in 1969, the Football Day came to St. Rita and never left - a bond that has lasted 36 years. Alderman Burke, shown above in 1969 and in a more recent picture, was the second youngest alderman when elected to the Chicago City Council and is now the longest serving. As a part of the Chicago area Catholic education system all his life (Visitation, Quigley and DePaul), Alderman Burke has been a faithful friend to St. Rita; he is shown below addressing the crowd at the 1986 14th Ward Football Day at St. Rita's Stadium on 63rd & Claremont.

The original 14ᵗʰ Ward Regular Democratic Organization Football Day, which started in the 1950's, changed venue each year, until 1969. On October 26, 1969 the Annual Football Day for the group was held at St. Rita, then at their Stadium on 63ʳᵈ and Claremont; its been with St. Rita ever since, even moving to the new campus at 77ᵗʰ Street; the 14ᵗʰ Ward celebrated its 36ᵗʰ Football Day at St. Rita in 2004.

St. Rita Novena

Literally thousands have attended the annual Novena to St. Rita over the last one hundred years. Begun in a small Chapel in what became know as "Green Hall", the Novena has grown in wonder each year. Today, it is held in a more modern facility, but the wonder of it all remains.

The Novena to St. Rita always has been celebrated at the Chapel located with the High School; in the past that was on 63rd Street, and today it is at 77th & Western. But, where it is doesn't matter; what matters is the devotion so many people have for St. Rita. Shown above is the current Shrine to St. Rita; below is the Chapel at the High School at 77th Street. On the facing page, scenes from the old location at 63rd Street are shown.

The annual novena to St. Rita has been a fixture at the school since the beginning. In the early days, attendance was low, matching the population in the neighborhood. As the renown of St. Rita spread, the circle from which the Novena drew its worshippers grew. By the 1950's, attendance was SRO as people came from far-and-wide to pray and seek her intercession. At left is a picture of the statue of St. Rita decorated for the occasion of the novena. Below is an example of the procession into the Chapel at Green Hall during the 1950's, with the Honor Guard provided by the Knights of Columbus. A small boy can be seen with a cap on at left center in the picture; the boy's name was Bernard Danber and he was a member of St. Rita Parish; Bernard Danber would grow up to become Father Bernard R. Danber, O.S.A. and would lead the High School through its transition and move to 77th & Western.

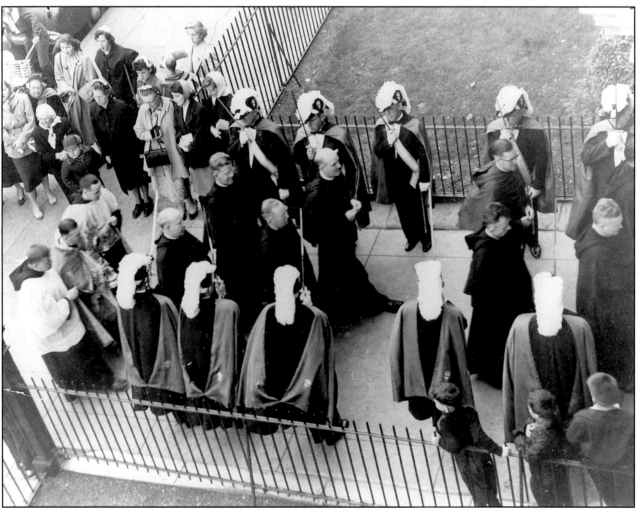

Spirituality

The Augustinian charism is to live a strong, healthy, Christian community. The Gospel invitation to TRUTH, UNITY, AND CHARITY motivates the entire St. Rita school community as we seek to love God and our neighbor, and enrich and develop our spiritual life. All-school Masses are celebrated monthly and on Holy Days, Family Masses quarterly. Seasonal liturgies are celebrated at Thanksgiving, Christmas, and Holy Week. The forgiveness of Christ is extended through celebrations of the Sacrament of Reconciliation throughout the year. Sacramental preparation is provided for students requesting it, and the Campus Minister is available for spiritual direction and pastoral counseling. Annual retreats are provided for all students, while Seniors participate in a four-day retreat experience called Kairos ("the Lord's Time"). Students play a role in St. Rita's Campus Ministry. They also serve as Lectors, Servers, and Eucharistic Ministers at school Masses. All students are required to complete 75 hours of community service (ROSE hours) as a prerequisite for graduation.

KAIROS RETREATS

While retreats have been a mainstay of St. Rita students' spiritual development for years, during the 1989/90 school year a new retreat program was introduced – Kairos retreats. Kairos is a time when students, with the help of their faculty leaders, come together and share their hopes and dreams and feelings. The purpose is to strengthen friendships and help each other on their journey through life. Through 2004/05, St. Rita seniors have been involved in 74 Kairos retreats. (The two photos at lower right show Kairos #'s 62 and 2 (at bottom)). The program is so successful that the St. Rita retreat leaders have reached out to other schools and helped them introduce their own retreat programs.

HALL OF FAME

St. Rita of Cascia High School sponsors its own Hall of Fame, to honor those individuals who have made a difference; many alumni, faculty and friends have been elected to the Hall over the years. Following is a list of these honored individuals.

St. Rita High School — Hall of Fame

John J. Cranley ('26) – Elected 1980
Edward W. Duffy ('80) – 1980
Nick Etten ('31) – 1980
Fr. James Green, OSA – 1980
Dennis Lick '72 – 1980
John J. Loftus ('44) – 1980
Fr. J. J. O'Malley, OSA – 1980
Raymond Parello ('45) – 1980
Louis A. Ricci ('53) – 1980
Hon. William J. Campbell ('22) – 1981
Fr. Francis P. Crawford, OSA – 1981
Leo Deutsch ('33) – 1981
Earl F. Evans ('30) – 1981
Bernard G. Badke ('35) – 1982
John F. Brice ('29) – 1982
Desmond Coleman – 1982
Thomas W. Dower ('10) – 1982
Fr. John J. Harris, OSA – 1982
John C. Egan ('60) – 1982
John R. Byrne ('64) – 1983
John J. Connelly – 1983
Fr. Thomas Nash, OSA – 1983
Terrence J. O'Reilly ('28) – 1983
Fr. Paul Potter, OSA – 1983
Fr. Joseph Coyne, OSA – 1984
Maurice "Pat" Cronin – 1984
Andrew "Bud" Gardner ('26) – 1984
John J. Madigan ('34) – 1984
William "Billy" Marek ('72) – 1984
John Orr ('36) – 1984
Fr. John Seary, OSA – 1984
Charles Brodnicki ('27) – 1985
Dr. Joseph Eraci ('51) – 1985
James Clancy ('74) – 1985
George Janky ('66) – 1985
Dr. Robert Keeley ('27) – 1985
Donald J. Senese ('60) – 1985
Hon. Edward Barrett ('17) – 1986
Dr. John Brosnan ('32) – 1986
Royal Bricker ('76) – 1986
Carl Cronin ('27) – 1986
Judge William Daly ('15) – 1986
Dr. James Gardner ('29) – 1986
John Jemilo ('48) – 1986
Hon. Walter Kozubowski ('57) – 1986
Fr. William P. Murphy ('33) – 1986
Coach Joseph Porreveecchio – 1986
Coach Thomas Shaughnessy – 1986

Arthur Shurlock ('55) – 1986
Fr. William Thomas, OSA – 1986
Thomas Burke – 1987
Fr. Leo Cavanaugh, OSA – 1987
Dr. Anthony Cutiletta ('59) – 1987
Donald Doody ('44) – 1987
Ed Farmer ('67) – 1987
Fr. Lavern Flach, OSA – 1987
Kenneth Jaksy ('52) – 1987
Ray Manczarek ('56) – 1987
Jack McHugh ('47) – 1987
James Miller ('47) – 1987
Fr. John Peck, OSA ('51) – 1987
Fr. Raymond Ryan, OSA ('48) – 1987
Joseph Scanlon ('58) – 1987
Ralph Steinbarth ('45) – 1987
Fr. Edward Chapman, OSA – 1988
Fr. Ruellen Fink, OSA – 1988
Edward Galvin – 1988
Raleigh W. Kean ('30) – 1988
Fr. William Lion ('49) – 1988
Dr. John Moran ('56) – 1988
John O'Toole – 1988
Kenneth Schuster ('44) – 1988
Col. Theodore Baadar ('45) – 1989
Coach Edward Buckley – 1989
Judge James Griffin ('29) – 1989
Dr. Casimir Firlit ('57) – 1989
Edward C. Novak ('51) – 1989
Joseph F. Bamberger – 1990
William T. Doyle ('41) – 1990
Francis P. Geralts ('38) – 1990
Dr. Donald Racky, Jr. ('54) – 1990
Edmund J, Rooney ('42) – 1990
Robert D. Cadieux ('55) – 1991
A. J. "Whitey" Cronin ('21) – 1991
Bernard J. Echlin ('36) – 1991
Mark P. Zavagnin ('79) – 1991
Thomas Maurice Frost ('40) – 1992
Edward A. Hoerster ('59) – 1992
Fr. Joseph B. Kepperling, OSA – 1992
Patrick E. Mahoney ('54) – 1992
Charles J. Zettek ('44) – 1992
Robert Zimny ('40) – 1992
John "Joker" Brady ('26) – 1993
Florian Dodge – 1993
Eugene McGrail ('41) – 1993
Fr. Walter McNicholas, OSA ('44) – 1993

Arthur Velasquez ('56) – 1993
Robert A. Black ('40) – 1994
Hon. Raymond Jagielski ('71) – 1994
Dr. Larry Sullivan ('62) – 1994
John Buckley ('70) – 1995
Fr. John J. FitzGerald, OSA – 1995
Dr. Michael Kisicki ('69) – 1995
William Lang ('32) – 1995
Jim Segredo ('73) – 1995
Fr. Robert Sheridan ('35) – 1995
Michael Sullivan ('64) – 1995
Fr. John F. Casey, OSA – 1996
Donald Petkus ('58) – 1996
Dr. Michael N. Riley ('68) – 1996
William B. Furlong ('45) – 1996
Br. Bob Fisher, OSA– 1997
Joe Lacny, Sr. – 1997
James Misiora ('67) – 1997
Br. James Small, SJ ('40) – 1997
Dr. John T. Tarpey ('43) – 1997
Fr. David L. Brecht, OSA – 1998
Kenneth Dodge ('72) – 1998
Fran Napleton ('43) – 1998
Mrs. Mary Thompson – 1998
Kenneth Danz – 1999
Len Strazewski ('72) – 1999
Fr. Gerard Theis, OSA – 1999
Fr. John Gavin, OSA ('40) – 2000
William Ivers ('41) – 2000
John Husar ('55) – 2001
Dennis Lucas ('66) – 2001
Mel Schreier ('28) – 2001
William Sims ('42) – 2001
Coach Barney Badke ('35) – 2002
Richard Hochgraver ('71) – 2002
Bob Jemilo ('53) – 2002
Harold J. Sheedy ('55) – 2002
Jerry Trandel ('52) – 2002
Dr. Joseph Gowgiel ('44) – 2003
Ben Reilly ('47) – 2003
John Piccione ('51) – 2003
Mike McArdle ('54) – 2003
Todd Wernet ('75) – 2003
Ronald Abramowicz ('60) – 2004
Russell Bugan ('44) – 2004
John Hoerster ('67) – 2004
Thomas O'Connell ('44) – 2004
Michael Schneider ('46) – 2004

ST. RITA OF CASCIA BOARD OF DIRECTORS

Province of Our Mother of Good Counsel

Very Rev. David L. Brecht, O.S.A., *Prior Provincial*
Rev. Thomas R. McCarthy, O.S.A., *President and Principal*, St. Rita of Cascia High School

Province Counselors

Rev. Christopher L. Howe
Rev. Bernard C. Scianna ('83)
Rev. Theodore E. Tack
Rev. R. William Sullivan
Rev. Philip C. Cook
Rev. William E. Lego

St. Rita Of Cascia High School
Board of Advisor Members 2003-2004

Ronald M. Abramowicz ('60)
Gary R. Baumgarten ('58)
Anthony C. Colosimo ('63)
John J. Curtin ('58)
Rev. Bernard Danber, O.S.A. ('68)
Sally E. Deenihan
Larry M. Doyle ('68)
James J. Gardner, O.D. ('29)
Michael Georgopulos ('72)
Patrick Graber
Thomas Harrington ('74)

Richard Hochgraver ('71)
Patrick E. Mahoney ('54)
Frank C. Mainczyk ('56)
Michael J. McArdle ('54)
Rev. Thomas R. McCarthy, O.S.A. ('83)
James C. Miller ('47)
Bryan J. O'Connor ('70)
Donald A. Petkus ('58)
Edward J. Schmit ('63)
Michael B. Schneider ('46)
Robert Wilson

Mothers' Club Officers

Maureen Wagner	President
Peggy Brooks	Vice President
Laura Carpenter	Treasurer
Therese Fitzgibbon	Corresponding Secretary
Laura Benson	Recording Secretary

Fathers' Club Officers

Charlie Yerkes	President
Dennis Lick	Vice President
Paul LoMaglio	Secretary
Patrick McCarthy	Treasurer
Jim Fitzgibbon	Financial Secy
David Ladd	Sergeant at Arms

St. Rita Of Cascia High School
Academic And Administrative Staff
2004-2005

Faculty

Michael Allocca, *Latin and Religious Studies*
    B.A. Columbia University
    M.A. University of Chicago
Jim Angsten, *Physical Education*
    B.A. Western Illinois University
    M.Ed. University of Illinois
Thomas Berry, *Social Studies*
    B.A. DePaul University
John Bonk ('75), *Business*
    B.A. Illinois Benedictine College
    M.A. Chicago State University
Dan Carroll, *Physical Education*
    B.S. Northeast Missouri State University
    M.A. Northeast Missouri State University
Paul Cooney, *Science*
    B.S. Governors State University
Brendan Coughlan, *Mathematics*
    B.S.A.E. Notre Dame University
Kathleen Curran, *Mathematics*
    B.S. Northern Illinois University
Fr. Bernard Danber, O.S.A. ('68), *Mathematics*
    B.A. Illinois Benedictine College
    M.Div. Catholic Theological Union
    M.Ed. Loyola University
Sally Deenihan, *Mathematics*
    B.A. Mundelein College
    M.A. St. Xavier University
Martha Dion, *Social Studies*
    B.A. St. Joseph's College
Ryan Egan, *Science*
    B.S. Northern Illinois University
Robert Gasiecki, *Science*
    B.S. Western Illinois University
Cindy Gradek, *Music-Band*
    B.A. DePaul VanderCook School of Music
Richard Grill ('64), *Technology*
    B.S. Chicago State University
    M.A. Governors State University
Br. Jack Hibbard, O.S.A., *Activities Director*
    B.A. Tolentine College
Br. Gary Hresil, O.S.A. ('86), *Religious Studies*
    B.A. St. Xavier University
    M.Div. Catholic Theological Union
Shaun Johnson, *Religious Studies*
    B.S. University of Wisconsin
Stan Kastelic ('78), *Social Studies and Religious Studies*
    B.A. Aurora College
Patrick Kelly, *Technology*
    B.A. St. Norbert
    M.S. Dominican University
Michael Kisicki, *English*
    B.A. Lewis University
    M.Ed. University of Arizona
    M.Ed. University of Arizona
    Ed.D. Loyola University
Chuck Knibbs, *Social Studies*
    B.A. Illinois State University

Susan Krystof, *Science*
    B.S. University of Illinois
    M.L.S. Dominican University
Robyn Kurnat, *Fine Arts*
    B.S. Illinois State University
Todd Kuska ('90), *Science*
    B.S. St. Xavier University
Danielle Lange, *French*
    B.A. Academie of Nancy, France
    M.Ph. Universite of Nancy, France
Norb Lasky ('60), *Mathematics*
    B.S. Loyola University
Antoine Leason, *Religious Studies*
    B.S. St. Xavier – Louisiana
    M.Div. Catholic Theological Union
Linda Marach, *English*
    B.A. Rosary College
    M.A. Northeastern Illinois University
Fr. Thomas McCarthy, O.S.A. ('83), *President/Principal*
    B.A. Villanova University
    M.Div. Catholic Theological Union
    M.A. Lewis University
Judy McGovern, *Spanish*
    B.A. University of Illinois
Jodi McLawhorn, *Music-Band*
    B.A. DePaul VanderCook School of Music
Antonio Miranda, *Religious Studies*
    B.A. Loyola Marymount
John Nee ('93), *English*
    B.A. University of St. Francis
Brian Opoka, *Mathematics*
    B.S. Quincy University
Brian O'Sullivan, *English*
    B.A. St. Xavier University
Maureen Pangrazio, *Science*
    B.A. St. Xavier University
David Parolin, *English*
    B.A. Loyola University Chicago
Joseph Partacz, *Mathematics*
    B.A. St. Xavier University
Greg Pawlowski ('61), *French and Spanish*
    B.A. University of Illinois
    M.A. Loyola University
Thomas Rohn, *Latin and Social Studies*
    B.A. Knox College
    M.A. University of Illinois
Dawn Scianna, *English*
    B.A. Dominican University
Jay Standring, *Religious Studies and Physical Education*
    B.A. Notre Dame University
    M.S. Chicago State University
Woody Urchak, *Physical Education*
    B.S. DePaul University
    M.S. University of Illinois
    Ph.D. University of Florida - Nova
Allison Weissman, *Spanish*
    B.A. Emory University
Nancy Zenere, *Mathematics*
    B.S. Chicago State University

ST. RITA OF CASCIA HIGH SCHOOL
ACADEMIC AND ADMINISTRATIVE STAFF
2004-2005

ADMINISTRATIVE & SUPPORT STAFF

Fr. Thomas McCarthy, O.S.A. (83), *President and Principal*
Sally Deenihan, *Vice President for Academic Affairs*
Fr. Wes Benak, O.S.A. ('81), *Assistant Principal*
Patrick Kelly, *Asst. Principal for Professional Development*
John Bonk ('75), *Athletic Director*
Br. Jack Hibbard, O.S.A., *Activities Director*
Fr. Bernard Danber, O.S.A. ('68), *Prior*
Joe Partacz, *Dean of Men*
Mary Barnes, *Dean's Office - Attendance*
Antoine Leason, *Campus Minister*
Bro. Jerome Sysko, O.S.A. *Campus Ministry*
Michael Patton, *Business Manager*
Anne Russell, *Registrar*
Robyn Kurnat, *Director of Professional Development*
Paul Harrington, *Director of Technology*
John Quinn ('87), *Director of Recruitment*
Joan Straple, *Development Office*
Trish Harrington, *Development Office*
Peggy Strocchia, *Development Office*
Bob Quinn, *Development Office*
Letitia Olinger, *Business Office*
Marge Byrne, *Switchboard*
Sr. Campion Maquire, RSM, *Switchboard*
Noreen Kelliher, *Administrative Assistant*
Connie Johnston, *Data Center*
Dorothy Larkin, *Main Office*
Jill Nagel, *Counseling Office*
Michael McClorey ('83), *Cafeteria Manager*
Kitty Turkowski, *Cafeteria Manager*

COUNSELORS

Fr. Walter McNicholas, O.S.A. ('44), Freshman
    B.A. Villanova University
    S.T.L. Pontifical Gregorian University, Rome
Jeffrey Timms, Sophomore/Junior
    B.A. Ohio State University
Fr. Wes Benak, O.S.A. ('81), Junior/Social Worker
    B.A. Villanova University
    M.Div. Catholic Theological Union
    M.SW. Loyola University
Sr. Mary Alice Hoff, OP, Junior/Senior
    B.A. Siena Heights College
    M.A. DePaul University
    M.A. Lewis University

ATHLETICS & ACTIVITIES STAFF

John Bonk ('75), Head Coach Basketball
Dan Carroll, Head Coach Wrestling
Paul Cooney, Head Coach Track
Kathleen Curran, Head Coach Bowling
Craig Ferguson, Head Coach Ice Hockey
Patrick Hughes, Head Coach Soccer
Stan Kastelic, Head Coach Golf
Chuck Knibbs, Head Coach Cross Country, Swimming
    and Water Polo
Todd Kuska ('90), Head Coach Football
Jill Nagel, Head Coach Volleyball
Mike Zunica, Head Coach Baseball
Jackie Bellam, Cheerleading
Cindy Gradek, Music and Band
Br. Jack Hibbard, O.S.A., Student Council
Joseph Partacz, Scholastic Bowl

SECURITY

Mary Bickham
Dave Brandt
Tim Clancy
Al Grzyb
Dan Hoffman
Chris Kane
Don Keevers
Don Larisey
Russ Marrella
Jim Meehan
Dan Nesis
Mike Rimkus
Tim Uldrych

CAFETERIA

Shawn Capporelli
Denise Gaylord
James Kucera
Shirley Lopez
Dorothy McKee
Lydia McNary
Therese Nielsen
Shirley Nizolek
Cathy Rice
Lil Yerkes

FACILITIES

Jim Gaylord
Don Jakubowski
John Ettawageshik
Pat Mitchell

BAND STAFF

Cindy Gradek
Jodi McLawhorn
Ken Danz
Rob Denty
Julie Tendy
Joel Martinez

Mrs. Sally Deenihan   *Fr. Wes Benak*   *Mr. Patrick Kelly*

Augustinian Religious Who Taught at St. Rita of Cascia High School

Bro. Philip Adelsbach
Fr. Bernard Albers
Fr. Richard Allen
Fr. Edward Andrews
Fr. Robert Atwood
Fr. J. Owen Barry
Bro. Raymond Barth
Fr. John Barthouski
Fr. Carl Bauman
Fr. Wes Benak
Fr. John Beretta
Fr. David Brecht
Fr. Donald Brennan
Fr. James Brice
Fr. Edmund Burke
Fr. John Burkhart
Fr. Vincent dePaul Burnell
Fr. Joseph Burns
Fr. Robert Burns
Fr. Leonard Burt
Fr. Dominic Caniglia
Mr. Grahame Capp
Fr. Gregory Carnevale
Fr. Angus Carney
Fr. John Casey
Fr. Francis Cavanaugh
Fr. Leo Cavanaugh
Fr. Edward Chapman
Fr. Robert Chrupka
Fr. Stanley Cibulskis
Fr. James Clark
Fr. Francis Coan
Fr. J. Raymond Collins
Fr. Philip Cook
Fr. James Corrigan
Fr. Joseph Coyne
Fr. Francis Crawford
Fr. Edwin Crosby
Fr. William Cullen
Fr. W. Timothy Cuny
Fr. Bernard Danber
Fr. Dudley Day
Fr. William Deacy
Fr. Timothy Deeter
Fr. Joseph Derby
Fr. George DeMarco
Fr. Edwin Dickenson
Fr. Erwin J. Dodge
Bro. Charles Domagalski
Fr. William Donovan
Fr. William Doyle
Fr. Albert Durant
Fr. William Egan
Bro. Mark Emken
Fr. John Fagan

Fr. Francis Fenton
Bro. Edward Finch
Fr. Ruellen Fink
Bro. Joseph Fisher
Fr. John Fitzgerald
Fr. John Fitzmaurice
Fr. LaVern Flach
Fr. John Flaherty
Fr. James Flynn
Fr. John Flynn
Fr. Mortimer Foley
Fr. Philip Foley
Fr. Roland Follmann
Fr. Cornelius Ford
Fr. Emmett Flynn
Fr. John Gaffney
Fr. James Gallagher
Fr. Patrick Gallagher
Fr. John Galloway
Fr. Thomas Garrett
Fr. John Gavin
Fr. Dennis Geaney
Fr. John Gilman
Fr. Ralph Giovinetti
Fr. John Glennon
Fr. John Glynn
Fr. Ambrose Godsil
Fr. Edward Gorra
Fr. Edward Grace
Fr. Charles Grady
Fr. Joseph Graham
Fr. James Green
Bro. Daniel Gridley
Fr. Edward Griffin
Fr. Thomas Griffin
Fr. Edward Hamel
Fr. Eugene Leroy Hamilton
Fr. John Hammond
Fr. Donald Harkabus
Fr. John Harris
Fr. Clarence Hart
Fr. Leo Hart
Fr. Daniel Hartigan
Fr. Joseph Hartman
Fr. Edmund Hayes
Fr. Joseph Heney
Fr. Joseph Hennessey
Fr. Jerome Heyman
Bro. John Hibbard
Bro. Augustine Hickens
Fr. Joseph Hickey
Fr. William Hoffman
Fr. Anthony Hogan
Fr. Michael Hogan
Fr. Sidney Horne

Fr. Chris Howe
Bro. Gary Hresil
Fr. Ferdinand Jordan
Fr. Charles Juzaitis
Bro. Timothy Kazanova
Fr. Thomas Kelly
Fr. William Kelly
Fr. William Kenny
Fr. Joseph Kepperling
Fr. Edward Kersten
Fr. Martin Kessels
Fr. Thomas Kiley
Fr. Wilbert Kirk
Fr. Jerome Knies
Fr. J. Theodore Knoll
Fr. John Kret
Fr. Edwin Kuczynski
Fr. William Labadie
Fr. John Lambert
Fr. Alfred LaFleur
Fr. Edward LaMorte
Fr. Francis Lawlor
Fr. Robert Lawrence
Fr. Cornelius Lehane
Fr. John Lehane
Fr. Thomas Leo
Fr. Donald Lewandowski
Fr. James Lichtfuss
Fr. Lorenzo Lozano
Fr. James Lyne
Fr. John Mabarak
Fr. Richard Maher
Fr. Jerome Mahoney
Fr. John Mahoney
Fr. Ananias Malillos
Fr. Augustine Maloney
Fr. Peter Marron
Fr. Edward Marsh
Fr. Sylvester Martin
Fr. Arthur Maxwell
Fr. Edward May
Fr. Henry McArdle
Fr. John McCall
Fr. Joseph McCarthy
Fr. Thomas McCarthy
Bro. Christopher McCartney
Fr. James McCloskey
Fr. Bernard McConville
Fr. Robert McCoul
Fr. Joseph McDermott
Fr. Francis McDonnell
Fr. Thomas McGowan
Fr. Richard McGrath
Bro. Terrance McGuire
Fr. Clement McHale

Fr. John McLaughlin
Fr. Richard McNally
Fr. Walter McNicholas
Fr. Vincent Meaney
Fr. John Medina
Fr. Richard Meehan
Fr. John Molnar
Fr. Daniel Murphy
Fr. James Murphy
Fr. John P. Murphy
Fr. Michael Murphy
Fr. Patrick Murphy
Fr. Thomas Nash
Fr. William Neis
Bro. John Newton
Fr. Edward Novak
Fr. John O'Brien
Fr. Francis O'Bryan
Fr. Joesph O'Connor
Fr. Michael O'Connor
Fr. Joseph F. O'Malley
Fr. Joseph J. O'Malley
Fr. Charles O'Neill
Fr. Martin O'Neill
Fr. Thomas O'Neill
Fr. William O'Rourke
Fr. John O'Toole
Fr. Noel Omlor
Fr. Thomas Osborne
Bro. Frank Paduch
Mr. Charles Pall
Fr. Robert Pare
Fr. Peter Paul
Fr. Casimir Pazera
Fr. John Peck
Bro. John Perovich
Fr. Joseph Perry
Fr. Richard Plunkett
Fr. Mario Porreca
Fr. Paul Potter
Bro. Charles Prevender
Fr. William Reilly
Fr. F. Rodriguez
Fr. Louis Rongione
Fr. David Ryan
Fr. Raymond Ryan
Fr. John Sattler
Bro. Paul Scanlon
Bro. Bernard Scianna
Bro. Eberhart Schaeflein
Bro. Anthony Schander
Fr. Theodore Schmidtt
Bro. Robert Schurman
Bro. Michael Schweifler
Fr. John Seary

Fr. Joseph Senke
Bro. David Sharp
Bro. Martin Shaw
Fr. William Sheedy
Mr. John Shields
Fr. Charles Shine
Fr. John Shirley
Fr. James Simpson
Fr. James Sinnott
Fr. Michael Slattery
Fr. Martin Sobiesk
Bro. Francis Spalla
Bro. Lawrence Sparacino
Fr. Francis Starrs
Fr. C. Edward Stengel
Fr. Reinhard Sternemann
Bro. John Stobba
Bro. Patrick Strong
Bro. Angelo Sturn
Fr. Edward Sullivan
Fr. William Sullivan
Fr. Luke Sweeney
Bro. Jerome Sysko
Bro. Thomas Taylor
Bro. Mark Thedens
Fr. Gerald Theis
Fr. William Thomas
Fr. Aloysius Tierney
Fr. John Timms
Fr. John Toomey
Fr. Daniel Trusch
Fr. Ronald Turcich
Fr. Bernard Tyler
Fr. Jacek Tylzanowski
Fr. John Tyma
Bro. Jerome (Charles)
    VanAlstyne
Fr. John VanDerBeek
Fr. Leander VanLieshout
Fr. Norman VanSile
Fr. Thomas VanThienen
Fr. Gerald VanOverbeek
Fr. Robert Verstynen
Fr. Richard Voight
Fr. J.T. Wade
Bro. Raymond Wallenberg
Fr. Stanislaus Weinert
Fr. Raymond Wheeler
Bro. William Wiegel
Fr. Henry Wierman
Fr. Frederick Winn
Fr. Stephen Wroblewski

St. Rita Men
Vocations

Spirituality runs strong at St. Rita of Cascia High School and many students have used their education at St. Rita as a springboard to a religious vocation; a number joined the Order of St. Augustine, whether after graduation or recruited directly out of St. Rita to finish their high school at the minor seminary; others joined different religious Orders or became diocesan priests.

Alumni in the Order Of St. Augustine

Fr. Wes Benak ('81)
Fr. Robert Chrupka ('53)
Fr. James Corrigan ('57)
Br. John Currier ('61)
Fr. Bernard Danber ('68)
Fr. Edwin Dickenson ('15)
Fr. John Dowling ('60)
Fr. William Doyle ('24)
Fr. John Flaherty ('46)
Fr. James Flynn ('32)
Fr. Harold Fryermuth ('54)
Fr. John Gavin ('40)
Fr. Ambrose Godsil ('29)
Br. Albert Gorka ('55)
Fr. William Griffin ('55)
Fr. Donald Harkabus ('49)
Fr. Anthony Hogan ('56)
Fr. Michael Hogan ('47)

Br. Gary Hresil ('86)
Fr. Clarence Jass ('59)
Br. Fred Kaiser ('58)
Fr. Edward Kersten ('47)
Fr. John Lambert ('61)
Fr. Henry Maibusch ('46)
Fr. Thomas Martin ('61)
Fr. Thomas McCarthy ('83)
Fr. John McCutchen ('56)
Fr. Walter McNicholas ('44)
Fr. Richard Meehan ('54)
Fr. Patrick Murphy ('66)
Fr. William Murphy ('33)
Fr. Thomas Nash ('31)
Br. John Newton ('75)
Fr. Gerald Nicholas ('58)
Fr. John O'Flaherty ('46)
Fr. Dan O'Grady ('66)

Fr. John Ohner ('63)
Fr. William O'Rourke ('39)
Fr. Frank Paduch ('67)
Fr. John Peck ('51)
Fr. David Petraitis ('69)
Fr. Lawrence Puchalski ('57)
Fr. Raymond Ryan ('48)
Fr. John Sattler ('54)
Fr. Bernard Scianna ('83)
Fr. John Shirley ('51)
Fr. Martin Sobiesk ('47)
Fr. Frank Sullivan ('48)
Fr. John Szura ('58)
Br. Mark Thedens ('55)
Fr. Alfred Tripamer ('55)
Fr. Ronald Turcich ('48)
Fr. John Tyma ('49)
Fr. Gerald Van Overbeek ('53)

Recruited from St. Rita by the Order Of St. Augustine

Fr. Edward Andrews
Fr. Alfred Burke
Fr. Richard Daley
Fr. Lawrence Dore
Fr. Thomas Dullard

Br. Robert Fisher
Fr. John Flynn
Fr. Philip Foley
Fr. Karl Gersbach
Fr. John Mangold

Fr. James Murphy
Fr. Casimir Pazera
Fr. Lawrence Poetzinger
Br. John Stobba
Fr. Michael Wolan

Priests, Religious, Deacons and Ministers

Br. Juniper Bala, OFM ('50)
Rev. Edward Belsan ('76)
Fr. Joseph Beranek, OP ('42)
Br. Leon Beranek, OFM ('53)
Dn. Joseph Brady ('49)
Fr. Louis Broidy ('16)
Fr. William Browne ('60)
Dn. Irvin Bryce ('62)
Msgr. Stephen P. Buckley ('09)
Dn. John Bumbel ('68)
Fr. Francis Cadek ('17)
Br. Matthew Capodice, CP ('47)
Fr. George Cerny ('52)
Fr. Jerome Chicvara ('52)
Br. Thomas Courtney, OFM ('51)
Fr. Philip Coury, CM ('58)
Fr. Edmund Davern ('49)
Br. Isaiah (Matthew) Dwyer, MC ('80)
Dn. James Fitzgerald ('54)
Msgr. Malachy Foley ('15)
Fr. Edward Geiss ('57)
Fr. Edward Grotovsky ('53)
Fr. Michael Hurley ('34)

Fr. Victor Ivers ('38)
Br. James ('63)
Archbishop Job (R. Osacky '64)
Fr. John Keating ('25)
Fr. Thaddeus (John) Kennedy, OCSO ('45)
Fr. James King, CSC ('77)
Dn. Donald Kotwas ('50)
Rev. James Kress ('80)
Fr. Fred Kulovits ('47)
Dn. Bernard Kut ('54)
Fr. Joseph Lauro ('31)
Fr. William Lion ('49)
Fr. Leo Lyden, CSP ('15)
Fr. James Lyons, MSJ ('41)
Fr. Ronald Mahon, CPPS ('69)
Br. Peter Martin, CFC ('61)
Dn. Tom McCarthy ('53)
Fr. Lawrence McMahon, SSC ('31)
Dn. Romuald Morowszynski ('63)
Rev. James Moscato, ECA ('60)
Dn. Paul Neakrase ('62)
Fr. Vincent Nels ('30)
Fr. William O'Brien ('20)

Msgr. Martin O'Day ('28)
Fr. Luke Ouska ('25)
Mr. Richard Ralphson, SJ ('92)
Rev. Denardo Ramos ('57)
Msgr. Tom Reidy ('59)
Fr. Joseph Reikas ('27)
Fr. Edward Ryan ('45)
Mr. Peter Sarolas ('87)
Dn. Kenneth Schoenfeld ('56)
Dn. James Sejba ('53)
Fr. Robert Sheridan ('34)
Br. James Small, SJ ('40)
Fr. Edward Stockus ('48)
Fr. Raymond Tillrock ('59)
Fr. Boniface Vaisnoras, MIC ('37)
Fr. Louis Vanderley, OSB ('53)
Msgr. Thomas Vidra ('51)
Fr. Gerald Walling, SJ ('46)
Dn. Eugene Wedoff ('45)
Fr. Amideus Wickers, OSM ('34)
Fr. Donald Wright ('44)
Fr. Richard Young, OFM ('82)
Dn. Ronald Yurcus ('62)

St. Rita Men
Who Gave Their All

World War I

While exact numbers are lost from School records, we believe six St. Rita graduates gave their all during World War I.

Howard Callahan ('13)   Robert Kennedy ('14)
Henry Grimes   James McCune ('11)
Robert Houlihan   Arthur O'Neil ('16)

World War II

Over 1,600 St. Rita men fought for their Country during World War II; in doing so, 53 died.

M. Baldwin ('41)   E. Grygienc ('41)   W. Mihalovich ('34)
N. Becker ('43)   T. Hannafin ('42)   R. Nugent ('33)
S. Beizis ('41)   G. Hanus ('41)   J. O'Connell ('33)
E. Bondi ('44)   B. Harlin ('42)   A. Odrowski ('43)
S. Botowic ('41)   W. Hession ('36)   T. Ouska ('31)
W. Boyd ('41)   J. Hogan ('28)   L. Rea ('41)
R. Braun ('43)   A. Hybiak ('43)   D. Rees ('42)
J. Caulfield ('38)   R. Jaske ('42)   J. Reid ('40)
J. Clement ('43)   A. Kokoefer ('43)   D. Ryan ('38)
P. Conway ('41)   R. Koscelnak ('38)   F. Schafer ('40)
E. Corcoran ('35)   P. Krause ('42)   G. Scully ('40)
J. Cronin ('35)   R. Krull ('42)   W. Sheehan ('35)
R. Davis ('43)   N. Lake ('35)   C. Sides ('36)
G. Doney ('43)   J. Madigan ('38)   J. Siera ('42)
J. Fedigan ('33)   W. Maine ('38)   T. Slattery ('43)
D. Foley ('42)   A. Mancini ('41)   S. Sorich ('34)
L. Gaik ('38)   J. McWilliams ('41)   J. Stenzel ('38)
E. Globis ('39)   G. Mersch ('42)

Korean War

R. Altosino ('43)   J. Pavlak
J. Andrasko ('50)   L. Piorunski ('43)
P. Gallagher ('47)   Q. Reidy ('48)
J. Hronic ('44)   J. Ritter ('48)
R. McLaughlin ('47)   J. Sokol ('50)

Vietnam War

J.C. Curtin ('65)
W. Frossard ('68)
G.J. Hlavacek ('64)
C.J. Hoban ('66)
D.J. Klimas ('64)
R.E. Liberty (60-63)
F.A. Pape ('65)
D.S. Pazdan ('60)
R. Reiche ('64)
R.J. Solczyk ('62)

This page reports all known graduates of St. Rita who died serving the United States during armed conflicts over the last 100 years. If we missed any, please let us know in the Development Office and we will correct the listing in subsequent printings.

St. Rita Fathers' Club
Presidents

1930/31 Mr. John Cook	1955/56 Mr. Emil DeLaura	1980/81 Mr. Don Taylor
1931/32 Mr.	1956/57 Mr. Emil DeLaura	1981/82 Mr. John Brown
1932/33 Mr.	1957/58 Mr. Jim Velette	1982/83 Mr. John Brown
1933/34 Mr.	1958/59 Mr. Walter Urbaniak	1983/84 Mr. Fran Pendergast
1934/35 Mr.	1959/60 Mr. Charles Satarino	1984/85 Mr. Edward Kendra
1935/36 Mr.	1960/61 Mr. Edward Stahl	1985/86 Mr. Donald Wojtowicz
1936/37 Mr. Paul Krause	1961/62 Mr. Felix Waisnoras	1986/87 Mr. Donald Wojtowicz
1937/38 Mr. William O'Keefe	1962/63 Mr. Anthony Chobot	1987/88 Mr. Thomas Schmidt
1938/39 Mr.	1963/64 Mr. James Pape	1988/89 Mr. Thomas Schmidt
1939/40 Mr. R.J. Clarke	1964/65 Mr. Frank Salvatori	1989/90 Mr. Richard Anderson
1940/41 Mr. John Rees	1965/66 Mr. Florian Kosinski	1990/91 Ric Yniguez/Tom Code
1941/42 Mr.	1966/67 Mr. Steve Zahr	1991/92 Mr. Joseph Eppolito
1942/43 Mr.	1967/68 Joe Heeney/Ed Poetz	1992/93 Mr. Robert Powers
1943/44 Mr.	1968/69 Mr. Stan Marek	1993/94 Mr. Mike Johnston
1944/45 Mr.	1969/70 Mr. Stan Marek	1994/95 Mr. Cesare Micheletto
1945/46 Mr.	1970/71 Mr. Erwin Thomas	1995/96 Mr. Cesare Micheletto
1946/47 Mr. James Sherry	1971/72 Mr. Charles McLaughlin	1996/97 Mr. Bill Cavanaugh
1947/48 Mr. Carroll Miller	1972/73 Mr. Stan Marek	1997/98 Mr. Bill Cavanaugh
1948/49 Mr. George Polka	1973/74 Mr. John Schumacher	1998/99 Mr. Sye Majka
1949/50 Mr. Clarence Mauer	1974/75 Mr. John Shea	1999/00 Mr. Sye Majka
1950/51 Mr. Harry Williams	1975/76 Mr. Bill Burnette	2000/01 Mr. Charles Yerkes
1951/52 Mr. Harry Williams	1976/77 Mr. Bill Burnette	2001/02 Mr. Bob Fitzgibbon
1952/53 Mr. Donald Steele	1977/78 Mr. Mark Sarich	2002/03 Mr. Paul Lomaglio
1953/54 Mr. Ray Manczarek	1978/79 Mr. Mike Egan	2003/04 Mr. Charles Yerkes
1954/55 Mr. Emil DeLaura	1979/80 Mr. Don Taylor	2004/05 Mr. Charles Yerkes

St. Rita Mothers' Club
Presidents

1930/31 Mrs. Agnes Coppinger	1955/56 Mrs. Ann Stalzer	1980/81 Mrs. Pat Foody
1931/32 Mrs. Agnes Coppinger	1956/57 Mrs. Dolly Schifferl	1981/82 Mrs. Pat Foody
1932/33 Mrs. Agnes Coppinger	1957/58 Mrs. Kay Thome	1982/83 Mrs. Marge McCormick
1933/34 Mrs. Agnes Coppinger	1958/59 Mrs. Mary Gomoll	1983/84 Mrs. Marge McCormick
1934/35 Mrs. Agnes Coppinger	1959/60 Mrs. Adelaide Sabath	1984/85 Mrs. Chris Gucwa
1935/36 Mrs. Agnes Coppinger	1960/61 Mrs. Josephine Barbaro	1985/86 Mrs. Chris Gucwa
1936/37 Mrs. Albert Jarvis	1961/62 Mrs. Florence Brady	1986/87 Mrs. Rosalie Nunez
1937/38 Mrs. Agnes Coppinger	1962/63 Mrs. Rinnie Barrett	1987/88 Mrs. Rosalie Nunez
1938/39 Mrs. Agnes Coppinger	1963/64 Mrs. Gert Marczewski	1988/89 Mrs. Bonnie Krol
1939/40 Mrs. Agnes Coppinger	1964/65 Mrs. Flo Zeeb	1989/90 Mrs. Maureen Curtin
1940/41 Mrs. Hermanek	1965/66 Mrs. Rita Kazmer	1990/91 Mrs. Maureen Curtin
1941/42 Mrs. Johnson	1966/67 Mrs. Lorraine Kipp	1991/92 Mrs. Linda Zettergren
1942/43 Mrs. Viola Kunzendorf	1967/68 Mrs. Irene Manfredi	1992/93 Mrs. Mary Young
1943/44 Mrs. Viola Kunzendorf	1968/69 Mrs. Marion Callinan	1993/94 Mrs. Mary Young
1944/45 Mrs. Ann Dobry	1969/70 Mrs. Evelyn Pavilionis	1994/95 Mrs. Toni Windt
1945/46 Mrs. G.R. King	1970/71 Mrs. Inez Cappel	1995/96 Mrs. Alice Porfirio
1946/47 Mrs. Eleanor Black	1971/72 Mrs. Mary Lou Seivert	1996/97 Mrs. Alice Porfirio
1947/48 Mrs. Mary Harvey	1972/73 Mrs. Pearl Mulvihill	1997/98 Mrs. Carol Angiollo
1948/49 Mrs. Hazel Nilles	1973/74 Mrs. Pearl Mulvihill	1998/99 Mrs. Alice Porfirio
1949/50 Mrs. Ann Schatz	1974/75 Mrs. Phyllis Parello	1999/00 Mrs. Sylvia Paprzyca
1950/51 Mrs. Marge Lassen	1975/76 Mrs. Norma Wendling	2000/01 Mrs. Sylvia Paprzyca
1951/52 Mrs. Adaleen Milas	1976/77 Mrs. Joan O'Malley	2001/02 Mrs. Shellye Pechulis
1952/53 Mrs. Marion LaFause	1977/78 Mrs. Kay Gorman	2002/03 Mrs. Sue Vaci
1953/54 Mrs. Victoria Soltis	1978/79 Mrs. Anne Russell	2003/04 Mrs. Maureen Wagner
1954/55 Mrs. Nancy Burns	1979/80 Mrs. Angel Bacarello	2004/05 Mrs. Maureen Wagner

Centennial Activities

Honorary Chairmen

Mr. Joseph F. Bamberger
43-year Teacher and 13th Principal
Rev. Thomas R. McCarthy, OSA ('83)
President/Principal

Honorable Edward M. Burke
Alderman 14th Ward
M.Rv. Robert F. Prevost, OSA
Prior General, the Vatican

Committee Members
Executive Committee

Fr. Tom McCarthy, O.S.A. ('83)
Dennis Lucas ('66)

Thomas Harrington ('74)
Peggy Rourke

Reception & Open House
James and Noreen Reilly

Ad Book & Dinner Dance
Dennis ('66) and Denise Lucas

Centennial Book
Rick and Jane Bessette

Arts & Graphics
Tim McCarthy ('85)
Eric Cronin ('97)

The Gala Champagne Toast
Jay (Hon) and Julie Standring

Block Party
Bob ('72) and Karen Jilek
Jack ('77) and Kathy Nagle
Pat and Michelle Platt
Mike and Kim Patton

Theme Parties - Chairs
Paul (Hon) and Nancy LoMaglio

The Cascia Canteen Party
Brian ('70) and Cathy O'Connor
Dave and Meg Wear

The Brick Wall Sports Bar Party
Gary and Diane Gallik
Tim and Liz Shanahan

The Mustang Round Up Party
Tom and Marge Hopkins
Mike and Julie Blake

Chinese Raffle
Jim and Trish Spratte
Steve and Beth Witczak

St. Patrick's Day Parade
Jay (Hon) and Julie Standring

Centennial Calendar Events

March 14, 2004
South Side Irish
St. Patrick's Day Parade

August 28, 2004
St Rita Family Block Party
Mass at 4:00 pm
Party on Grounds

January 29, 2005
Winter Homecoming
Cascia Canteen – 6:30 to 10:00
Brick Wall Sports Bar – 6:30 to 10:00
Mustang Round Up – 6:30 to 10:00
Gala Toast – 10:00 to Midnight

August 11-14, 2005
Centennial Celebration Weekend
Thursday – Ray Manzarek Concert
Friday – Golf Outing
Saturday – Hilton Chicago Dance
Sunday - Mass and Open House

Centennial Celebration Pictures

St. Rita High School, along with its extended family and friends, celebrated the 100th Anniversary of its founding by Father James Green in a series of events. In March, 2004 St. Rita was the Special Honoree in the Southside Irish St. Patrick's Day Parade; in August, 2004 St. Rita threw a Block Party for over two thousand. In 2005 there were two major event-weekends: January was Homecoming with three Theme Parties and, second, a Centennial Weekend in August where a Golf Outing, a concert featuring St. Rita's own rock and roll legend Ray Manzarek from the *DOORS* (with the Larkin Brothers as the opening act), a Hilton-Chicago Ball and a Mass with Open House brought festivities to a resounding finish.

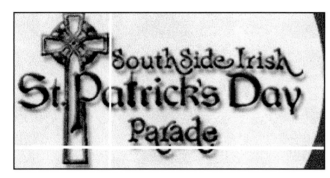

CONTRIBUTORS

A memorial book such as this requires the help and participation of many people: friends, alumni, heirs, contributors and a whole range of interested parties. Central to this effort was the Development Office members, especially Peggy Strocchia and Trish Harrington, two ladies who are so loyal to St. Rita they even married Ritamen; thanks also to Noreen Kelliher in the President's Office. Thanks go out to the Chicago Historical Society, the Cardinal Bernardin Archives and Records Center of the Archdiocese of Chicago, and the Augustinian Archives in Villanova, Pennsylvania. We also wish to thank all the members of the various Centennial Activity committees who worked on so many projects for this celebration. Following is a list of some of the people who contributed photographs, interviews, artifacts and their time and talent. We apologize if we missed anyone.

Michael Allocca
Lee Ann Arethas (for Don Mrozek ('65))
Louis Beuschlein ('56)
John Bonk ('75)
The Brady Family
John R. Byrne ('64)
David Castro ('71)
Jim Clark ('67)
David Cromer (Fenwick hockey)
Fr. Bernard Danber, O.S.A. ('68)
Sally Deenihan (Hon)
Martin Doorhy ('73)
Larry Doyle (for Bill Doyle ('41))
John Egan ('60)
Mrs. Earl Evans (for Earl ('29))
John Flaherty ('70)
Patrick Flannery ('66)
John Foley ('86)
Dr. Jim Gardner ('29)
Joan Gergits (Alderman Burke's Office)
Rich Grill ('64)
Fr. Daniel Hartigan, O.S.A.
John M. Hartigan (for Tom Dower ('10))
John Herlihy ('83)
Br. Jack Hibbard, O.S.A. (Hon)
Miriam & William Hillmert ('24)
Ray Jagielski ('71)
Dave Johnson ('97)
Stan Kastelic ('78)
Mike Kisicki ('69)
Chuck Knibbs
Shirley Kosic (for Robert C. Braun '43)
Don Kroitzh (Five Corners Press)
Dennis Lick ('72)
Joyce Lugo (for John Brown)
John Madigan ('34)
Tim Maher ('71)

Pat Mahoney
Mike Maione ('56)
Bill Marek ('72)
Fr. Thomas McCarthy, O.S.A. ('83)
Peggy McKenzie (for Ernie Mrozek ('71))
Fr. Walter McNicholas, O.S.A. ('44)
Rob Medina (Chicago Historical Society)
Ed Merrion (for Joseph Merrion ('16))
Jim Miller ('47)
Mary Misiora (for Jim Misiora ('67))
Mike Murtagh (Hon)
Tom Noone (Associated Design)
Julie Morris (for George O'Brien ('16?))
Mike O'Grady ('48)
Red Pastorek ('58)
Mike Patton
Paul Petriekis ('58)
Jim Porrevecchio ('70)(for Coach Joe)
Curtis Price ('88)
Jim Prunty (Hon)
Quality Plus Photo (Worth)
Peggy Rourke
Anne Russell
Julie Satzik (Chicago Archdiocese Archives)
Mary Beth Sheehan
Fr. John Sheridan, O.S.A.
James Schreier (for Mel Schreier ('28))
Ken Schuster ('44)
Jim Segredo ('73)
Br. Lawrence Sparacino, O.S.A. (Hon)
Anthony Studin ('45)
Larry Sullivan ('62)
Br. Jerome Sysko, O.S.A.
Br. Tom Taylor, O.S.A.
Jaclene Tetzlaff (Chicago Sun-Times)
Art Velasquez ('56)
Mark Zavagnin ('79)

Along with our Thanks comes a pre-emptive Apology. Works such as this covering 100 years are impossible to get perfect. If you see any errors (of omission or commission) or misspellings, please let us know in the Development Office and we will correct it in any subsequent printings. Thanks to all.

Works Consulted

Bibliography:

Causland, Robert H. *A Tale to Tell, A Time to Remember.* Tennessee Valley Publishing, Knoxville, 1999.

Cavanaugh, Francis J., OSA. Editor in Chief and Publisher. *The Augustinians, Our Mother of Good Counsel Province, Twenty-Fifth Anniversary, 1941 – 1966.* American Yearbook Publishing.

Headley, Kathleen J. *Chicago Lawn/Marquette Manor.* Images of America Series. Arcadia Publishing, Chicago, 2001.

Koenig, Harry, editor. *A History of the Parishes of the Archdiocese of Chicago.* Catholic Bishops of Chicago, Chicago, 1980.

Montay, Sister Mary Innocenta, CSSF. *The History of Catholic Secondary Education in the Archdiocese of Chicago.* Catholic University of America Press, Washington, D.C., 1953.

Pruter, Robert. *Catholic High School Basketball Tournaments.* Elmhurst, Illinois. <http://www.ihsa.org/feature/hstoric/cathtour.htm>

Secardo, Joseph, OSA, translated from Spanish by Dan J. Murphy, OSA. *Life of Sister St. Rita of Cascia.* D.B. Hanson & Sons, Chicago, 1916.

PREP BOWL, Commemorative Book 1934-1999. Chicago Tribune Company, Chicago, 2000.

Websites:

I.H.S.A. sports records: <http://www.ihsa.org>

Chicago Archdiocese Archives: <http://www.archives.archchicago.org>

Thom Ryng ('84) e-article: <http://www.livejournal.com/users/thomryng/5945.html>

St. Rita Original Documents:

1975/76/77/78/79/80/81/82/83/84 St. Rita Ice Hockey Ad Book

1975 (1st)/76/77/78/79/80/81/82/83/84/85/88/89/92/93/94/96/99 (25th)/00/01/02/03/04 Ice Hockey Banquet Celebration Books.

12/75 (43rd Annual), 12/77 (45th Annual), 12/80 (48th Annual), 12/82 (50th Annual), 12/83 (51st Annual) St. Rita Football Banquet/Ad Books.

Handbook of St. Rita High School – 1940-41 school year (4th Edition), 1951-52 school year (15th Edition), 1966-67 school year (? Edition).

Remembering Our Forty-Four Years Of Augustinian Life…. St. Rita Monastery, Chicago, 1993.

St. Rita Yearbooks, 1931 to 2004; various issues of *Cascian* and *Ritan*, 1923 to 2004.

St. Rita Alumni Directory, Second Edition. St. Rita Alumni Association, 1963.

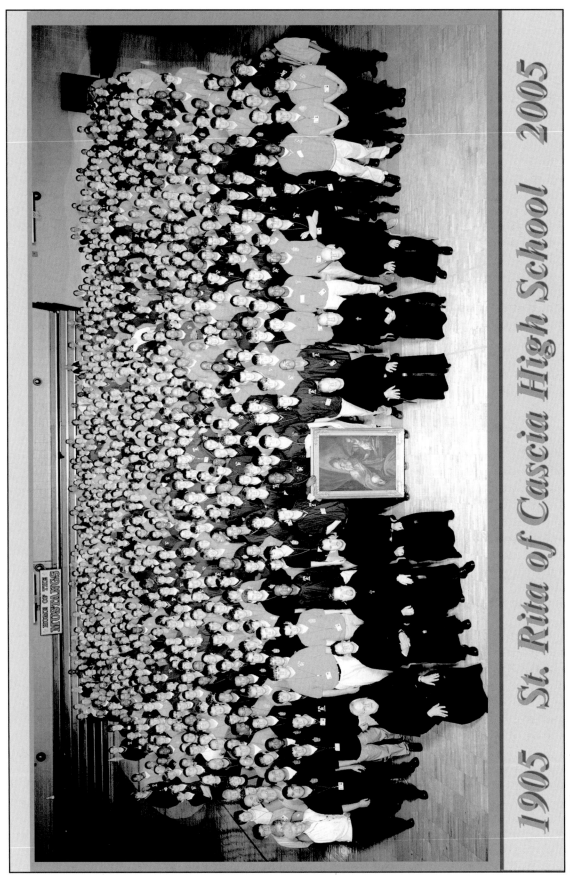

St. Rita of Cascia High School 1905 2005

Tom Killoran Photography